Collaborating to Meet Standards:

Teacher/Librarian Partnerships for K–6

Toni Buzzeo
MA, MLIS

Linworth
PUBLISHING, INC.

Library of Congress Cataloging-in-Publication Data

Published by Linworth Publishing, Inc.
480 East Wilson Bridge Road, Suite L
Worthington, Ohio 43085

ISBN 1-58683-023-6

5 4 3 2 1

Table of Contents

Collaborative Units

About the Author

About the Author

Toni Buzzeo is a practicing library media specialist at Longfellow Elementary School in Portland, Maine, as well as an author. She holds an M.A. from the University of Michigan in English Language and Literature and an M.L.I.S. from the University of Rhode Island. In 1999, she was named Maine Library Media Specialist of the Year by the Maine Association of School Libraries. As an educator, she has worked as a library media specialist for 14 years and previously taught both high school and college English. As a writer, she is the author of professional books for librarians and teachers as well as two forthcoming children's books. She is a frequent presenter at library, reading, and writing conferences. Her Web site, <www.tonibuzzeo.com>, offers additional insight into her many professional interests as well as her books. She can be reached at *tonibuzzeo@tonibuzzeo.com*.

Speaking Engagements

Librarians and educators who wish to contact Toni Buzzeo about conference and staff development speaking engagements related to Teacher-Librarian collaborations may visit her Web site at <www.tonibuzzeo.com>.

Acknowledgments

I wish to thank my wonderful library media specialist contributors and their collaborative teaching partners for their generosity in sharing these collaborations, for countless hours of work in preparing their units for publication, and for having the good grace always to look for one more content standard, performance indicator, resource, or rubric to round out their contributions.

Dedication

To all of the administrators who have encouraged collaboration and to all of the teachers who have collaborated with me throughout the years, at Congin, Margaret Chase Smith, Lyseth, Reiche, Baxter, and Longfellow Schools. And especially to Eunice Gilbert, the first to believe in a new vision of library instruction, and Marty Miller, who continues to stretch my thinking farther than I ever thought it possible to stretch.

Introduction

Since the publication of *Information Power: Building Partnerships for Learning* in 1998, we library media specialists have a "collaboration" mandate: "Collaboration for authentic, information-based learning—through shared planning, teaching, collection development, and management strategies—provides the model for all the program's connections to the larger learning community (American Association of School Librarians 123)." But, some wonder, is *collaboration* just the latest buzzword "consultation" once was? Is there likely to be a new word, a new mandate, just around the information literacy bend?

Buzz words. We all know them, speak them, write them, sometimes even resent them. A few years ago, in the Longfellow School Library Media Center in Portland, Maine, where I am Library Media Specialist, a colleague brand new to the staff interrupted a schoolwide curriculum development meeting to complain. "What does all that mean?" she demanded.

"All what?" we asked, stupefied.

"All that jargon."

Ahhh, I thought, the buzz words. Words such as *learner expectations*, *content standards*, *key learnings*, *benchmarks*, *summative* and *formative assessment*, and yes, *collaboration* were flying around the room. I wondered, "Is collaboration just another educational buzz word, or is it the clarion call in the wilderness of information literacy instruction?"

Organizational "private-speak" can be a tool to improve communication on the inside but also to exclude those on the outside. *Collaboration* is a different sort of term. While it is a buzz word in educational circles, especially in library media specialist circles, it is also a word that carries the same meaning in the larger world: the world of politics, both national and international, the world of business, the world of community affairs, the world of family. At every level of human interaction, we collaborate for the benefit of all members of the group.

As a library media specialist with a career-long commitment to collaboration, I have sought the opportunity to envision, plan, and teach in partnership with my colleagues—whether classroom teachers or other specialists, administrators, or public librarians—to meet the learning goals and standards identified for student achievement. Collaboration is a perfect means to address local, state, and national standards in education in order to achieve student learning. In fact, collaboration has aided not only in achieving standards, but also in raising scores on standardized tests, another source of concern and occasional stress in the teaching profession. Standardized tests assess both declarative and procedural knowledge. In the library media center, we team with our colleagues to teach both content and process. Students, then, carry away not only content knowledge but also procedural knowledge and are able to apply their understanding to questions they encounter on local, state, and national assessments.

In recent years, as I attended countless collaboration workshops at countless library conferences (workshops stuffed to the hallways and spilling into them), it occurred to me that as a group, library media specialists were hungry for knowledge and assistance in collaborating. We wanted information. We wanted suggestions for overcoming roadblocks. We wanted practical, easily adoptable and adaptable units that worked!

And so the idea for this book was born. *Collaborating to Meet Standards: Teacher/Librarian Partnerships for K–6* is written for practicing elementary library media specialists and their teaching partners. It is intended to be a guide in our endeavor to satisfy the 1998 *Information Power* mandate. In addition to a roundup of opinions, research, and philosophy from the library literature—and from working library media professionals— about collaboration, which is essential to your understanding of the mandate, you will find useful and practical suggestions for its implementation and its impact. Most important of all, however, the primary focus of this book is a collection of wonderful units written in a standardized template that you can borrow, adapt, and use in your own collaboration efforts.

You will find three, meaty introductory chapters. Chapter One is a history of cooperation and collaboration in school libraries over the past decade. Chapter Two examines the definitions and benefits (to administrators, to teachers, to library media specialists, and above all, to students) of collaboration and the studies that have proven its value, quantitatively. In Chapter Three, you will read about the factors necessary for success and the keys to overcoming roadblocks, including the stories of many practicing library media specialists who have struggled and succeeded with sticky scheduling problems, resistant teaching partners, and challenging school cultures. You will learn that, if necessary, you can even work with restrictions! And you will, I hope, become convinced that collaboration is not just a buzzword, but a goal worth striving for, a concept that offers benefits for library media specialists, teachers, students, and administrators. An index will allow you to search the concepts and ideas in these introductory chapters.

Following the introductory chapters, you will find a common template for use in planning collaborative units. It is clear, comprehensive, and easy to use. Finally, you will find a wealth of collaborative units contributed by library media specialist-and-teacher teams all over the United States. They are examples of best work, best thinking, best practice.

So step forward with me to the tune of the marching drum and heed the clarion call. Information literacy awaits!

Resources

American Association of School Librarians and Association for Educational Communications and Technology. *Information Power: Building Partnerships for Learning*. Chicago: American Library Association, 1998.

Chapter One

Collaboration: Where We've Been— Where We're Going

Setting the Stage

Picture this:

Date: May 2000
Cast: A class of fifth graders each clutching an audiobook and a sheet of notebook paper, a fifth grade teacher, a library media specialist
Scene: Longfellow School Library Media Center, Portland, Maine. Tables arranged in a "U" shape. Microphone set up at the apex of the tables. Guidelines for good audio reviewing posted on an easel. Video camera running.

The teacher and the library media specialist, who have team planned and team taught this language arts unit, begin by delivering their own audio reviews, then sit amidst the students as one after another stands and makes his or her way to the mike. There, each student shares an audio review, painstakingly revised in response to feedback from the teaching partners, with an audience of peers. The following day, in the same setting, and with rules posted for participation, the students and teaching partners engage in a round table discussion of the umbrella question, "Is listening reading?" as it applies to their "reading" of audiobooks during the month-long project. Excitement crackles in the air both days, especially when the celebratory cake is cut. After the crumbs are cleaned up and the class is sent off to physical education, the teacher and library media specialist meet to congratulate each other on their success and refine both the unit and the rubric in anticipation of a repeat performance next year. This unit is a definite "keeper."

Now turn the clock back nearly a century:

Date: 1904
Cast: A class of high school juniors, their English teacher, the school librarian, one of the first appointed professionally trained school librarians in the United States.

Scene: Library, Girl's High School, Brooklyn, New York. Long oak library tables, a Victrola on a corner table, leatherbound sets of poetry neatly lined up on mahogany shelves.

Unlike the collaborating library media specialist just described, whose job, as we know it, is defined by the criteria of expert teacher, instructional partner, information specialist, and program administrator, this librarian occupies the more traditional "keeper of the books" role.

She sits behind a circulation desk in a single reading room of approximately 3,000 volumes, lined up in perfect order. The English teacher leads his class through the door and nods cordially but cursorily at the librarian. His students follow him to the Victrola in the corner of the room. Seated at the long library tables, they listen to the recordings of English songs that the librarian has carried across the room to the teacher. At the teacher's prompting, students listen for elements the songs have in common with lyric poems they have been studying. Before the class leaves the library, the librarian comes forth to remove the brand new reference book, *The Columbia Grangers's Index to Poetry*, from the locked glass case where it is housed with other valuable reference books. She instructs the group in the use of the index, then retreats to the circulation desk to check out student selections made from the leather bound sets of poetry by Keats, Wordsworth, and Shelley. As the class leaves the library, the English teacher once more nods at the librarian, this time a bit more graciously, and thanks her for her assistance (Hall 627).

New Roles

By the mid-twentieth century, the role of the librarian as "keeper of the books" had begun to change. AASL standards published in 1960 and 1969 contributed to this change, and by 1975, the publication of the AASL standards, *Media Programs: District and School*, identified two instructional roles: design and consultation (AASL 6). As a designer of instruction, the librarian was charged with initiating and participating in curriculum development. As a consultant, the librarian was to recommend media applications for instruction (Pickard n. pag.).

The Taxonomies

By 1982, the three elements of the library media program—traditional library services, audiovisual services, and instructional development—combined to create a new view of the role of the library media specialist (Loertscher, "The Second Revolution" 417). A variety of models for instructional development and design began to appear in the literature simultaneously with the first publication of Loertscher's library media specialist taxonomy in 1982. Collaboration had arrived on the school library horizon and has held sway in library literature ever since!

The 2000 revision of the taxonomy, published in *Taxonomies of the School Library Media Program*, 2nd edition, included ten levels of involvement.

The Library Media Specialist's Taxonomy
by David V. Loertscher
1. **NO INVOLVEMENT**
   The Library Media Center (LMC) is bypassed entirely.
2. **SMOOTHLY OPERATING INFORMATION INFRASTRUCTURE**
   Facilities, materials, networks, and information resources are available for the self-starter delivered to the point of need.

3. **INDIVIDUAL REFERENCE ASSISTANCE**
   The library media specialist serves as the human interface between information systems and the user.
4. **SPONTANEOUS INTERACTION AND GATHERING**
   Networks respond 24 hours a day and 7 days a week to patron requests, and the LMC facilities can be used by individuals and small groups with no advance notice.
5. **CURSORY PLANNING**
   There is informal and brief planning with teachers and students for LMC facilities or network usage—usually done through casual contact in the LMC, in the hall, in the teacher's lounge, in the lunch room, or by e-mail. [For example: Here's an idea for an activity/Web site/new materials to use. Have you seen . . .? There's a software upgrade on the network.]
6. **PLANNED GATHERING**
   Gathering of materials/access to important digital resources is done in advance of a class project upon teacher or student request.
7. **EVANGELISTIC OUTREACH/ADVOCACY**
   A concerted effort is made to promote the philosophy of the LMC program.
8. **IMPLEMENTATION OF THE FOUR MAJOR PROGRAMMATIC ELEMENTS OF THE LMC PROGRAM**
   The four LMC program elements—collaboration, reading literacy, enhancing learning through technology, and information literacy—are operational in the school. The LMC is on its way to achieving its goal of contributing to academic achievement.
9. **THE MATURE LMC PROGRAM**
   The LMC program reaches the needs of every student and teacher who will accept its offerings in each of the four programmatic elements.
10. **CURRICULUM DEVELOPMENT**
    Along with other educators, the library media specialist contributes to the planning and organization of what will actually be taught in the school or district (Loertscher 17).

In his February 1982 *Wilson Library Bulletin* article, "The Second Revolution: A Taxonomy for the 1980s," Loertscher emphasized the merits of each level, saying there was no need for guilt. He felt that the first necessary step was to accept the entire list as a collection of legitimate roles of instructional involvement, each level being "good" (417–418).

Yet, the higher one goes on the taxonomy, the more collaborative is the relationship between teacher and library media specialist. While Mary might have hovered between Levels One and Four, it is Levels Eight through Ten that hint at and then extend the role of "instructional consultant" first introduced in the 1988 AASL *Information Power: Guidelines for School Library Media Programs* document (26). In other words, as Pickard pointed out in 1994, we were advised by our professional organization to stop being reactive, as described in Levels Three through Eight, and become proactive, as required by Levels Nine and Ten (n. pag.).

National Library Power Program

In 1988, through the National Library Power Program, the DeWitt Wallace-Reader's Digest Fund granted monies to New York City Public Schools to create library programs that improved the quality of education. By 1998, the program had been implemented at 19 sites (700 schools) nationwide serving more than one million children with an investment of over $40 million.

Collaborative planning was a major focus of Library Power professional development training sessions. In fact, the Library Power grant required that a site establish a totally flexible library program that employed collaborative planning. The fourth of six goals was to "Encourage collaboration among teachers, administrators, and librarians that results in significant improvement in the teaching and learning process" ("National Library Power Program" n. pag.). Rusty Taylor, Lead Library Media Coordinator of Wake County Public Schools Media Services and formerly Library Media Coordinator at the Aldert Root Elementary School, a Library Power school in Raleigh, North Carolina, says:

> Although funding from our Wake Education Partnership ended in 1998, we definitely have a Library Power legacy. When we started the Library Power program, only 7 of our 55 elementary schools had flexible access [a key factor in ensuring collaboration in elementary schools]—this year, we have 75 elementary schools, and 65 now have flexible access—yet the actual four years of DeWitt Wallace funding affected only 20 of our elementaries (n. pag.).

According to Butt and Jameson, Library Power "became a formidable driving force for initiating and continuing support for professional collaboration between library media specialists and their classroom teachers" (n. pag.).

Collaboration and Information Power

In a decade, the three roles of the library media specialist from *Information Power: Guidelines for School Library Media Programs*—information specialist, teacher, and instructional consultant (26)—had grown. By 1998, when *Information Power: Building Partnerships for Learning* was published, four roles were recommended—teacher, instructional partner, information specialist, and program administrator (4–5). The old "instructional consultant" role had been replaced with the updated term "instruction and curriculum partner." The "consultant" role of the 1988 document was outdated, inferring an unequal status, with the library media specialist more qualified than other teachers on the planning team (Muronaga and Harada 9). Partnership, on the other hand, implies equal status and participation.

Library Media Specialist Nancy Witte-Meredith of Carl Allgrove School, R.D. Seymour School, and East Granby Middle School in East Granby, Connecticut, who considers herself an instructional partner rather than a consultant, explains the differences.

> I see an instructional consultant as someone who leads one through a new process, teaching a new skill or instructional design. Instructional partners, on the other hand, learn from each other and both contribute experience and inspiration to the project. We each contribute from our strengths and skills, and the result is more effective than solo efforts (n. pag.).

Collaboration and Job Descriptions

State education departments and district central offices have taken up the charge in defining the teaching partner role of the library media specialist. In Wisconsin, the Department of Public

Instruction identifies content standards for initial and professional licensure of library media specialists. In both Communication and Group Dynamics, where the candidate can "Initiate and sustain collaborative instructional partnerships with teachers and other staff," and in Instructional Leadership, where the candidate can "Collaborate with teachers in teaching and evaluating instructional activities," there is a focus on the current collaborative role as defined by AASL ("Library Media Specialist Licenses" n. pag.). Likewise, West Hartford (Connecticut) Public Schools defines the role of the library media specialist in this way: "Library media specialists play an essential role in the learning community by collaborating with teachers, administrators and others to prepare students for the communication age" ("Library Media Services" n. pag.).

The New Frontier

Nor is it only library literature singing the praises of collaboration! Collaborative practice has become the focus of education at large. Teamwork for the purpose of improving instruction and student learning is being touted by top educational consultants and theorists. In 1998, when Wiggins and McTighe, assessment experts, set forth their Understanding by Design planning model in a book of the same title, they bemoaned lack of time for collaborative planning:

> Historically, U.S. education has minimized the role of planning and design in
> teaching. The frenetic pace of daily school schedules, the demands of nonteach-
> ing duties, and the general lack of time reserved for planning (within and
> beyond the teaching day), make it difficult for educators to engage in substan-
> tive curricular planning and design work, especially with colleagues (158).

Furthermore, school improvement consultant Mike Schmoker devotes his entire first chapter of *Results: The Key to Continuous School Improvement* to 'Effective Teamwork,' desig-nating collaboration as one of his three key components that favor results and improvement in schools. "We must acknowledge," he writes, "that schools would perform better if teachers worked in focused, supportive teams (10)." The focus, he says, must always be on student achievement. "Everyone in the educational community must work diligently to change the struc-tures that impede teamwork. But meanwhile, we must take advantage of the opportunities that already present themselves—and which others have demonstrated can eventuate in better results (11)."

So the age of collaboration has, indeed, arrived. We've experienced a change of enor-mous proportions throughout education and, in particular, in school librarianship—from Mary's quieter, dustier decade to these lively collaborative years of the new millennium. With our new mandate, vision, and skills, we're delving, alongside our teaching partners, into collaborative instructional design and delivery. This is clearly school librarianship's new frontier.

Resources

American Association of School Librarians and Association for Educational Communications and Technology. *Information Power: Building Partnerships for Learning*. Chicago: American Library Association, 1998.

American Association of School Librarians and Association for Educational Communications and Technology. *Information Power: Guidelines for School Library Media Programs*. Chicago: American Library Association, 1988.

American Association of School Librarians, American Library Association, and Association for Educational Communications and Technology. *Media Programs: District and School*. Chicago: American Library Association, 1975.

Butt, Rhonda and Christine Jameson. "Steps to Collaborative Teaching." *Wisconsin Association of School Librarians*. 3 February 2002 <http://www.wla.lib.wi.us/wasl/Steps%20to%20Collaborative%20Teaching%2(19-32).pdf>.

Hall, Mary E. "The Development of the Modern High School Library." *Library Journal* 40 (September 1915): 627.

"Library Media Services." *West Hartford Public Schools*. 23 July 2001 <http://www.whps.org/library/>

"Library Media Specialist Licenses." *Wisconsin Department of Public Instruction; Instructional Media and Technology*. 19 July 2000. <http://www.dpi.state.wi.us/dltcl/imt/lmslic.html>.

Loertscher, David. "The Second Revolution: A Taxonomy for the 1980s." *Wilson Library Bulletin* 56 (February 1982): 417–421.

Loertscher, David V. *Taxonomies of the School Library Media Program*. 2nd ed. San Jose: Hi Willow Research & Publishing, 2000.

Muronaga, Karen and Violet Harada. "The Art of Collaboration." *Teacher Librarian* 27:1 (October 1999): 9–14.

"National Library Power Program." *American Library Association*. 21 Feb. 2001. 4 Aug. 1998 <http://www.ala.org/aasl/libpower/>.

Pickard, Patricia W. "Current Research: The Instructional Consultant Role of the School Library Media Specialist." *SLMQ* 21:2 (Winter 1993). 18 Sep. 2000 <http://www.ala.org/aasl/SLMR/slmr_resources/select_pickard.html>.

Schmoker, Mike. *Results: The Key to Continuous School Improvement*. 2nd Ed. Alexandria, Virginia: Association for Supervision and Curriculum Development, 1999.

Taylor, Rusty. Personal interview. 11 Feb. 2001.

Wiggins, Grant and Jay McTighe. *Understanding by Design*. Alexandria, Virginia: Association for Supervision and Curriculum Development, 1998.

Witte-Meredith, Nancy. Personal interview. 11 Feb. 2001.

Chapter Two

Collaboration: How It Looks and Who It Benefits

Examining the Definitions

What IS collaborative planning? Recall the audiobook review project from Chapter One, and we can draw some conclusions. First, collaborative planning is two or more equal partners who set out to create a unit of study based on content standards in one or more content areas plus information literacy standards, a unit that will be team-designed, team-taught, and team-evaluated. Or, as the Nebraska Educational Media Association (NEMA) defines it, "Collaborative planning is teachers and library media specialists working together as an instructional team to plan for instruction that integrates information literacy skills and resources with curriculum objectives" ("Collaborative Planning" n. pag.).

There has been some confusion since the 1980s, however, over the differences among three related concepts—cooperation, coordination, and collaboration. In *Collaboration*, a document in the ALA Learned Lessons series, Grover makes the point clearly. While in cooperation, the teacher and library media specialist work independently but come together briefly for mutual benefit, their relationship is loose. Coordination means there is a more formal working relationship and an understanding of shared missions. The teacher and library media specialist do some planning and communicate more. However, in collaboration, the two partners have a prolonged and interdependent relationship. They share goals, have carefully defined roles in the process, and plan much more comprehensively (2). Applying Loertscher's taxonomy, cooperation happens at Levels Three, Four, and Five; coordination happens at Levels Six and Seven; and collaboration begins with Level Eight, with full implementation at Level Nine (*Taxonomies of the School Library Media Program* 17).

Donham provides a comprehensive and visionary definition of that work at Level Ten:

> When teachers and library media specialists work together to identify what students need to know about accessing, evaluating, interpreting, and applying information; when they plan how and where these skills will be taught and how they relate to content area learning; when they co-teach so students learn the

skills at a time when they need them; and when they assess the students' process as they work with information as well as the end product, they have truly collaborated (21).

The library media specialist-teacher team is an educational gift. The library media specialist has familiarity with a broad range of resources as well as expertise in information skills and strategies, and the teacher has intimate knowledge of both the students and the content area. Pair them closely as equal partners from the inception of a unit through its execution and assessment, and the partners, the school community, and the students are the lucky beneficiaries of the union.

Assessing the Benefits

So, what are the many benefits of the new collaborative model? Much attention has been justifiably afforded them in the professional literature. In *Collaboration*, Grover (7) lists ten global benefits of collaboration:

- Students are move involved in learning, and their work is more creative.
- Collaboration "ignites" creativity among teachers, and the "creative fire" spreads to learners.
- Modeling collaboration results in more collaboration among faculty in the school.
- Modeling collaboration influences students, teachers and parents, who learn to share ideas.
- Teachers, principals and librarians communicate more frequently.
- When students work in teams, the role of the teacher changes to that of resource person and learning facilitator.
- When students work in groups, the student's role changes also.
- Students learn to interact with people outside of the school.
- The library media program is integral to the collaborative teaching model.
- Administrators benefit professionally from their participation in teaching teams.

The Nebraska Education Media Association (NEMA), on the other hand, focuses more closely on the outcomes of collaborative planning ("Collaborative Planning" n. pag.). They assert that collaborative planning:

- promotes student achievement;
- promotes library media centers as central to the learning environment;
- promotes innovative instructional design;
- strengthens critical thinking and problem solving skills;
- provides opportunities for interaction between library media specialists and teachers;
- promotes sharing of resources;
- promotes integration and instruction of information literacy skills with the curriculum;
- enhances relevant use of all resources in all formats;
- provides opportunities for teachers to be aware of available resources;
- promotes intellectual freedom and equitable access to information and ideas; and
- strengthens connections with the learning community.

Still another worthwhile view NEMA has taken of the advantages of collaboration is to look at the benefits to the various constituencies affected: administrators, library media specialists, teachers, and students.

Benefits to Administrators

Administrators benefit in a variety of ways from the collaborative planning of their teachers and library media specialists, as NEMA indicates. Beneficial instructional partnerships are developed, information skills goals and objectives are front and center and are integrated throughout the curriculum, the time and energy of the library media specialist is used effectively, and flexible scheduling is supported. All of this provides time for teachers and library media specialists to plan together as well as ensures that the library is utilized for comprehensive units addressing a variety of subject areas and content standards, often simultaneously.

Benefits to Library Media Specialists

Of course, collaboration benefits library media specialists too. It allows us to use our wide-ranging skills in instructional design, teaching, assessment, information consulting, and program planning and administration. We also have the chance to facilitate partnerships, integrate our information skills curriculum into content area instruction, promote the use of our many print and nonprint resources, and develop a dynamic facility that serves as the instructional heart of the school. As a side benefit, as Debra Kay Logan points out in her *Information Skills Toolkit*, collaboration leads students, teachers, and administrators to better understand the role, expertise, and responsibilities of the library media specialist (Logan 3). And, adds Witte-Meredith, "As an LMS, I learn more about each subject I collaboratively teach. I stretch and try new things. Sharing ideas and techniques improves my teaching. Teachers benefit in similar ways and feel supported (n. pag.)."

Benefits to Teachers

Teachers are also beneficiaries of the collaboration model. Through collaboration with the library media specialist, they have regular and practical opportunities to communicate their resource needs to the library media specialist, to practice resource-based instruction using a wide variety of resources, and to integrate information literacy into their content area instruction. In addition, partnering with the library media specialist lightens the load on the classroom teacher and makes teaching both more interesting and more effective. As Dorcas Hand, Librarian at Annunciation Orthodox School in Houston, Texas, says, "For teachers, the collaboration offers two heads to work out the project and two sets of eyes to supervise it (n. pag.)." Jill Brown, Library Media Specialist, Nardin Academy, Buffalo, New York adds, "We both share our strengths: the teacher knows the subject; I know the research strategies. The kids get the best of both worlds (n. pag.)."

Benefits to Students

By far, the most important benefits of collaboration fall upon the students lucky enough to be taught by collaborating teachers and the library media specialists. They learn independent use of relevant, integrated information skills, experience the excitement of resource-based learning, and have the advantage of at least two teachers for collaborative units. As Witte-Meredith points out, "Collaboration is energizing. It leads to active learning for students. Students learn to make new connections between subject areas, and their learning multiplies (n. pag.)."

And it is, after all, student learning and student achievement that schools are all about! We collaborate primarily because, as Donham asserts, we want learning to be meaningful, authentic, and applied (20). Assignments created by teachers and library media specialists in concert are more likely to be authentic, complex, and significant. Information skills are taught in the context of new and creative units of study. As a result, students benefit and achievement rises.

Keith Curry Lance and Student Achievement Studies

The ongoing work of Keith Curry Lance, director of the Library Research Service, a unit of the Colorado State Library operated in partnership with the University of Denver's Library and Information Services Department, and his associates affords the most significant evidence of the positive impact of collaboration on students—the impact on student achievement. Lance's 1993 study, now referred to as the "First Colorado Study," was published as *The Impact of School Library Media Centers on Academic Achievement*. In addition to size of expenditure, staffing levels, and collection size as determinants of student performance, this landmark study revealed that students whose library media specialists played an instructional role tended to achieve higher average test scores (92–93). This finding led to further study with even more significant results.

Lance's Alaska study, published in 2000 as *Information Empowered; The School Librarian as an Agent of Academic Achievement in Alaska Schools, Revised Edition*, also found an unequivocal link between school librarians and higher test scores, the impact increasing as levels of librarian staffing increase. In addition, this study also found that regardless of the level of librarian staffing, the more time library media staff devoted to delivering information literacy instruction, planning cooperatively with teachers, and providing inservice training to teachers and staff, the higher the student test scores (65–66).

Pennsylvania determined in 1999 to be the first state east of the Mississippi to undertake a study of factors in school library media centers that impact student achievement. The study, published February 2000 as *Measuring Up to Standards: The Impact of School Libraries & Information Literacy in Pennsylvania Schools* showed a positive relationship between Pennsylvania System of School Assessment (PSSA) reading scores and library staffing. In addition, the report detailed, "as library staffing, information resources and information technology rise, so too does the involvement of school librarians in teaching students and teachers how to find and assess information" (Lance 6). Finally, the study found that test scores increase as school librarians spend more time, among other things, **teaching cooperatively with teachers** (7).

The second Colorado study, published in 2000, *How School Librarians Help Kids Achieve Standards—The Second Colorado Study* carried the investigation even farther. It found that Colorado Student Assessment Program (CSAP) reading scores increased with increases in four library program traits. These include: program development, information technology, individual student visits to the library media center, and most interestingly, **teacher/library media specialist collaboration**!

> A central finding of this study is the importance of a collaborative approach to information literacy. Test scores rise in both elementary and middle schools as library media specialists and teachers work together. In addition, scores also increase with the amount of time library media specialists spend as in-service trainers of other teachers, acquainting them with the rapidly changing world of information (Lance 7–8).

All this research adds up to new and indisputable knowledge: school library media specialists, particularly those working in collaboration with teachers as teaching partners, have an impact on student achievement. Furthermore, as Ken Haycock says, "Collaboration between teacher and teacher-librarian not only has a positive impact on student achievement but also leads to growth of relationships, growth of the environment and growth of persons" (Haycock 38). Collaboration is, then, a benefit to every member of the school community.

Resources

Brown, Jill. Personal interview. 12 Feb. 2001.

"Collaborative Planning: Partnerships Between Teachers and Library Media Specialists." *NEMA-Nebraska Educational Media Association*. 20 July 2000 <http://nema.k12.ne.us/CheckIt/coplan.html>.

Donham, Jean. "Collaboration in the Media Center: Building Partnerships for Learning." *NASSP Bulletin* 83:605 (March 1999): 20–26.

Grover, Robert. *Collaboration*. Chicago: American Association of School Librarians, 1996.

Hand, Dorcas. Personal interview. 10 Feb. 2001.

Haycock, Ken. "Collaborative Program Planning and Teaching." *Teacher Librarian* 27:1 (October 1999): 38.

Lance, Keith Curry, Christine Hamilton-Pennell, and Marcia J. Rodney. *Information Empowered; The School Librarian as an Agent of Academic Achievement in Alaska Schools, Revised Edition*. Juneau: Alaska State Library, 2000.

Lance, Keith Curry, Lynda Welborn, and Christine Hamilton-Pennell. *The Impact of School Library Media Centers on Academic Achievement*. San Jose: Hi Willow Research & Publishing, 1993.

Lance, Keith Curry, Marcia J. Rodney, and Christine Hamilton-Pennell. *How School Librarians Help Kids Achieve Standards: The Second Colorado Study*. San Jose: IIi Willow Research & Publishing, 2000.

Lance, Keith Curry, Marcia J. Rodney, and Christine Hamilton-Pennell. *Measuring Up to Standards: The Impact of School Libraries & Information Literacy in Pennsylvania Schools*. Greensburg, Pennsylvania: Pennsylvania Citizens for Better Libraries, 2000.

Loertscher, David V. *Taxonomies of the School Library Media Program*. 2nd ed. San Jose: Hi Willow Research & Publishing, 2000.

Logan, Debra Kay. *Information Skills Toolkit: Collaborative Integrated Instruction for the Middle Grades*. Worthington, Ohio: Linworth Publishing, Inc., 2000.

Witte-Meredith, Nancy. Personal interview. 11 Feb. 2001.

3

Collaboration: The Ideal and Its Many Variations

Factors for Success

What factors determine success in the effort to implement collaboration in library media centers? The library literature offers plenty of answers. For instance, the Nebraska Educational Media Association (NEMA) lists 15 "Elements for Successful Collaborative Planning" ("Collaborative Planning: How It's Done" n. pag.):

- Administrative support
- Shared philosophy, vision and goals
- Flexibly scheduled library media center
- Student centered teaching and learning
- Shared decision making
- Available resources and staffing
- Professional partnerships and teaming
- Effective communication
- Respect
- Good instructional design
- Varied strategies for teaching and learning
- Roles that are flexible yet identified
- Staff development
- Time management
- Education

In *Collaboration*, Grover divides a similar list of 14 factors for success (which he terms "lessons") into six categories: Environmental Factors, Group Membership Characteristics, Process/Structure, Communication, Purpose, and Resources. However, it is his four lessons under "Environmental Factors" that will speak most meaningfully to individual school library media specialists adopting a collaborative model:

- Lesson 1. School culture must support collaboration.
- Lesson 2. Flexible scheduling is a vital component of collaborative planning and work.
- Lesson 3. The library media specialist can and should be a leader of the efforts to collaborate.
- Lesson 4. Expect apathy and/or dissent among faculty.

Add to that Lesson 9 under Process/Structure: "School administrators and other decision-makers must support the concept of collaboration" (Grover 3–5), and it's a pretty complete list of the essentials: school culture, favorable scheduling patterns, levels of trust and commitment in collegial relationships, and administrative support. Haycock notes that "the characteristics and actions of the people involved [are] most important" to collaborative planning ("Collaborative Program Planning and Teaching" 38). Witte-Meredith concurs, "An enthusiastic partner is the biggest plus" (n. pag.).

If Haycock is right, what strategies encourage positive characteristics and actions in the people involved? Berkowitz (n. pag.) offers several suggestions to the library media specialist:

- Be prepared to offer suggestions for consideration.
- Share your concerns openly and honestly.
- Clarify roles and responsibilities
- Focus on points held in common.
- Use humor.
- Provide open-ended suggestions.
- Be the "official" note taker and report back.

In addition, it is important to share common goals about what students will know and be able to do. Design-down instructional development models ensure that we begin with instructional goals, but in the absence of a design-down model, it is worth taking time to ensure that all members of the planning team agree on the desired student outcomes as well as the process.

Finally, much of the literature recommends the use of a planning form to ensure success. A form allows for efficient recording of goals, decisions, and responsibilities during planning sessions (recorded by the library media specialist, in Berkowitz's suggested "official" note taker capacity). The best planning forms are simple and straightforward, yet comprehensive enough to ensure that unit responsibilities, outcomes, and resources are clear and that the unit is easily replicable. The form on which the units in this book are recorded is one such template.

Overcoming Roadblocks to Success

The library literature reveals three major stumbling blocks: lack of administrative support, difficult scheduling patterns, and school culture/teacher resistance. One additional roadblock, lack of library media specialist interest, knowledge, or training, can also interfere. But we can often turn roadblocks around, work them to our advantage, and make them keys to success.

The Role of the Administrator

As you read these two experiences from practicing library media specialists, consider the ways that a principal can be a key to collaboration success. Jill Brown says:

> I have been in this position for eleven years. When I came, there had been no

librarian or library program, just a room with books. The principal who hired me gave me free rein, and there was no one there to tell me, 'We never did it that way before.' The current principal had been a middle school Language Arts teacher at this school prior to her appointment. She made extensive use of the library and, as a teacher, was always willing to try new things. She really bought into the idea of flexible scheduling and open access and no grades (n. pag.)

And Witte-Meredith says:

My principal is very supportive. He has provided substitutes to allow for teaching, dress rehearsal, and performance times. He is enthusiastic about the collaborative project and willing to problem solve with us. My assistant principal volunteered to wear a tuxedo and be the ringmaster in our "Carnival of Animals" performances (n. pag.)."

These four administrators provided strong support for collaboration by supporting a flexible schedule and open access, helping to problem solve, hiring subs to allow for planning time, participating in collaboratively taught units, and quite simply, getting out of the way and letting it happen. According to Haycock, research findings show that "Collaborative planning requires a knowledgeable and flexible teacher-librarian, with good interpersonal skills and a commitment to integrated information literacy instruction, and the **active support of the principal**" ("Collaborative Program Planning and Teaching" 38). In fact, he says, "The role of the principal is so critical to the development of school priorities, culture, and resources that it would be fair to say the principal is the key factor in developing an effective and integrated school library program."

What, then, are the ways a principal who understands the value of the collaborative model supports it? Chief among them are expectations. Van Deusen's 1993–94 AASL/Highsmith Research Award Study revealed that curriculum consultation was significantly higher when the principal expected teacher-librarian collaborative planning (Van Deusen n. pag.). This, of course, demands an administrator who is willing to offer strong leadership and take risks. He or she must be willing to design job descriptions, hire new teachers, and set goals with current faculty with explicit expectations for collaboration. "When an administrator asks classroom teachers how they are using the media center resources and the expertise of the teacher-librarian, the probability of collaboration between the teacher-librarian and classroom teachers is likely to increase" (Bishop and Larimer 20). In addition, principals can include collaboration expectations in evaluations, observe planning sessions between teachers and library media specialists, monitor and log collaboration events, and provide inservice instruction in collaboration (Donham 24).

For success, the principal must stay informed about collaborative planning and library media center usage through regular communication. In turn, the library media specialist must keep the principal informed by sharing the weekly schedule, preparing monthly reports, and inviting the observations of or participation in library media center learning activities. We must play our role in this process if we expect to garner the administrative support that collaboration requires.

Time and Scheduling

The issues of time and scheduling are the next big set of roadblocks to be overcome. Witte-Meredith claims, "Common planning time is the biggest roadblock. Our school has collaboration days and sometimes a partner and I can have a common planning time of one to two hours when substitutes are provided. Creative planning for before school, after school and lunch time meeting also help (n. pag.)." How can we overcome the huge roadblock of time? The solution points back to the administrator. Possible variations are many, but the task requires creativity by administrators, librarians, and teachers who value collaboration. And let's face it, sometimes it's just a matter of coming in early or staying late to meet and take the most important first step—planning.

The much larger hurdle of the two, however, is scheduling. If the school is bound to a full, lockstep, rigid schedule, not only is there not time for teachers and library media specialists to jointly plan, there is also not time for them to jointly teach and to delve into a unit in ways that sometimes require much more than a weekly visit for a fixed time period! The van Deusen study supported the assumption that "If library media specialists are not bound to full teaching schedules, the likelihood of their performing in a consulting role can increase" (n. pag.). How much more likely is the teaching partner role, then! Sue Myers, Library Media Specialist at Nitrauer Elementary School in Lancaster, Pennsylvania, agrees and laments:

> Even with success in collaboration, I still have some classes that I have not seen
> for a research class yet this year! The roadblocks to collaboration have been the
> number of students in the building and the rigid schedule that we must maintain
> in order to service our resource room children and Spanish immersion program
> (n. pag.).

Bishop and Larimer point out that "A number of factors help facilitate successful collaboration between teacher-librarians and classroom teachers. Probably the most important factor is flexible scheduling" (19). In fact, as Gniewek points out, flexible scheduling makes teacher-library media specialist planning essential (34). With no set pattern or design for library media center use, all units become collaborations. Becca Stith, Library Media Specialist at Mission Trail Elementary in Leawood, Kansas, couldn't agree more.

> In an elementary school setting, flexible scheduling is an integral part of the
> collaboration process. Students are better served when classroom teachers and
> the library media specialist combine their efforts to coordinate units in all areas
> of the curriculum (n. pag.).

Now consider the frustrations of fixed scheduling. Deborah A. Monck, Media Specialist at Meadow Park Elementary School in Port Charlotte, Florida, had seen positive results from her long-standing flexible schedule. However, a rigid schedule has now been enacted, and she and her program are feeling the pinch.

> Having a full-flexible schedule in my elementary library for the past nine years
> had given me the opportunity to provide a wide variety of library and learning
> experiences for our students. Classes could come in on an "as needed" basis
> and teachers could schedule any amount of time periods needed. I had the flexi-
> bility to attend their grade level meetings to plan units, lessons, grade level

activities and the like. I could work with the teachers and meet their needs, and spend the time necessary to meet their curricular objectives. Now, due to cuts in budget and staff, my program has been reverted to the rigidly fixed schedule, whereby I see each class for a 35- or 40-minute period once a week. At the release time for the teachers planning period, I can no longer meet with them during their team meetings. There is no time to plan units, entertain spontaneous visits, extend lessons, or any of the other wonderfully collaborative things that we've done in the past. While 'on the wheel' to provide the contractual break, and the limitations of a brief weekly visit which includes book checkout, I am finding it difficult to find teachers to collaborate or the time to do so (n. pag.).

Unfortunately, the library media center schedule is often not the library media specialist's decision. As Myers and Monck experienced, scheduling decisions happen elsewhere. Some library media specialists have found a mixed schedule to be the answer. Van Deusen's study shows that "occurrences of all five curriculum consultation variables [gather, identify, plan, teach, evaluate] were significantly greater in schools employing flexible or mixed scheduling than in schools employing fixed schedules" (19).

Such a mixed schedule is working for some library media specialists. Karen White, Librarian at Durham Elementary School in Durham, Maine, says:

We have fixed schedules for all classes and half of Monday and all day on Friday for flex scheduling. Fixed schedules do not always work, but because we are a (relatively) small school, we are able to work the fixed schedule so that most all collaborations can be worked out, especially with the all day Friday schedule available for middle school teachers to bring all classes into the library for extra research, etc (n. pag.).

Myers has also met with some success in using **a mixed schedule** in her elementary school.

We have a rigidly scheduled program with each K–5 class having a 20 minute lesson and 10 minute book exchange time each week (total 30 minute block). No classes are scheduled on Friday so that teachers may sign up for research times or special lessons. The flex Friday has really done wonders for collaboration (n. pag.).

Nevertheless, there are schools in which no flexibility in the library schedule is possible at all. Butt and Jameson claim that even in these situations, collaboration is possible. "While flex scheduling offers the most supportive scenario for collaboration by the library media specialist and the classroom teacher, success within a fixed schedule is still possible" (n. pag.). They note that in order for it to happen, the teacher and the library media specialist must pre-plan the lesson and the teacher come to the library media center with his or her students. In order for pre-planning to take place, they say, professional planning times must coincide.

School Culture

The third potential roadblock to teacher-library media specialist collaboration is school culture. When a school lacks a collaborative work culture, teaching partnerships and collaboration have nothing on which to build. Consider Farwell's formula for successful collaboration. "The most promising formula for successful information literacy instruction is a combination of an energetic, knowledgeable, open-minded, and committed library media specialist; a flexible, confident, team-oriented staff; a risk-taking principal who understands change, how to manage both people and budgets, and the advantages and needs of an integrated resource-based instructional program; and a system for providing regular, collaborative planning time during the school day" (30). Administrators, teachers, and library media specialists all must see collaboration as an effort worth a risk. The value of a collaborative climate in the school, then, cannot be underestimated!

In their article, "The Art of Collaboration," Muronaga and Harada agree. They begin by suggesting that the library media specialist must be willing to lead or to be an active team member as the situation requires (10). They outline eight steps to developing a collaborative culture: building trust, developing collaborative relations, creating leadership teams, planning interactive meetings, valuing strengths, varying roles and responsibilities, emphasizing team work, and viewing planning as a nonlinear, holistic, and dynamic process (10–14). Many of the contributors to this book share Muronaga and Harada's beliefs and experiences.

Building trust goes a long way toward encouraging further collaboration. Patricia Mahoney Brown, Library Media Specialist, has built trust with her teaching staff at Benjamin Franklin Elementary School in Kenmore, New York.

> It is most important and vital. We share various ideas and our knowledge on any particular issue and topic of learning. We bring to the partnership meeting various learning styles and try to address each style in the lessons developed, we evaluate each other's materials with kindness, we praise each other, we develop a respect for each other and closer bonds not only in teaching but also in friendship (n. pag.).

Developing collaborative relations over time is equally important. But how does the library media specialist do it? Ann van der Meulen, Library Media Specialist at West Street Elementary School in Geneva, New York, has this advice.

> Communication, mutual respect, pleasant persistence, and patience are critical. Having a sense of humor helps. Providing assistance and support when opportunities arise and building on experiences from one year to the next generates further collaborative activity. I try to take advantage of every opportunity to become involved in classroom initiatives, especially the seemingly small ones, to create a program nearly seamlessly connected (n. pag.).

Another useful enterprise is the creation of and participation in leadership teams. If the library media specialist steps forward when there are building or district initiatives, he or she will have an opportunity not only to participate but also to collaborate. This was true for White when statewide learning results were introduced. "The school culture is becoming more and more helpful to my efforts as the teachers work on the Learning Results and see how collaboration and research and libraries can work hand in hand (n. pag.)."

"In planning interactive meetings, librarians wishing to collaborate must allow for a variety of venues and be flexible," says Brown.

> We collaborate in different ways: at formal grade level meetings, at casual coffee get-togethers in the morning, lunch time in the faculty room, bumping into each other in the corridor, passing in monthly planning sheets to the library or most often a combination of some or all of these.... Part of the success of collaboration is our being flexible to do whatever is best for the teacher and her class (n. pag.).

Valuing strengths and acknowledging individual differences in our teaching partners is also important. Says Myers, "I often mentor new teachers, share ideas and teaching techniques with experienced teachers, and collaborate on lessons with everyone (n. pag.)."

In addition, it is important to be sensitive to the need for varying roles and responsibilities in collaborative partnerships. Hand says she is alternately a consultant and a collaborative partner, depending on the attitude of the teacher. "I do both, depending on the teacher's receptiveness to my contributions. I tend to consult with those who are just beginning to want library input, but to partner with those more aware of and willing to use integrated skills (n. pag.)."

Perhaps the underlying necessity in a collaborative school culture is an emphasis on teamwork. The library media specialist can become the cheerleader for team members' assumption of a variety of roles and responsibilities in the planning and execution of collaborative units. Abigail Garthwait, currently Assistant Professor of Education in Instructional Technology at the University of Maine and formerly Librarian of Asa Adams Elementary School in Orono, Maine, emphasizes supporting "the self-efficacy of the teachers—getting them to think outside of the box that [says] they are solely responsible for their students' education (n. pag.)."

Finally, it is important to remember that the planning process and the development of collaborative partnerships do not always proceed in a lockstep, linear fashion. Library Media Generalist Linda D. Sherouse, working at North Hampton School in North Hampton, New Hampshire, notes:

> Our school has been focusing on writing new benchmarks for each grade level as we try to refine and reduce the number of standards we teach to. This has caused an upheaval in curriculum and the shifting is causing some staff to try new units and to teach areas they have not taught before (n. pag.).

Working with Restrictions

But what if you have done all you can by way of developing a collaborative culture and there are still roadblocks ahead of you? How do you work with restrictions and still move forward? Establishing collaboration takes time. Haycock claims, "Changes as complex as collaborative program planning and team teaching that reflect different approaches to teaching and learning do not take place quickly or easily; they are evolutionary, usually over two to five years . . ." ("Fostering Collaboration, Leadership and Information Literacy" 83). What, then, to do in the two to five years of change? How do you use those years to your best advantage?

First, remember that trust is the bedrock of collaboration. The more trust you can engender in the teachers you hope to collaborate with, the more likely they are to meet you halfway. Here's how Brown started.

I picked out a couple of really interested and supportive teachers. We worked
together to plan 'neat stuff' so that the kids in other classes would start asking
their teachers when they were going to do the same thing. I went to meetings,
booktalked or displayed materials at faculty meetings. In other words, made
myself very visible. I would bend over backwards to accommodate requests if at
all possible (n. pag.).

Second, assess the comfort level of various teachers and match the collaborative activity
you suggest with that comfort level. Van der Meulen did this. She explains, "I began with the
people who were most receptive to the concept. Some interactions began very small and have
grown over the years. Others jumped in full-fledged and we continue to improve over time"
(n. pag.). So did Kristin McIntire, Library Media Specialist at Conners-Emeerson School in Bar
Harbor, Maine.

There were several teachers who already did projects with the library. Some of
them were quite in-depth, others were not. I offered to sit with the teachers to offer
them more support and resources (and to get suggestions for new purchases).
These rather informal meetings were opportunities to give suggestions for
improvement and to involve myself in the planning, teaching, and assessment.
I've found that teachers are happy to have help and appreciate the time that
specialists can offer (n. pag.).

Which leads me to a theory shared with me by my principal, Sheila Guiney, at the start
of my first professional school library job, at Margaret Chase Smith School in Sanford, Maine. I
was discussing the need to bring all staff members on board with flexible scheduling and collaboration. She told me that she'd been in a workshop many years before in which she'd learned a
theory that applied to every situation in which a group of people are asked to change. In every
group, she said, there will be three clusters, divided roughly into thirds. The first cluster is the
"Oh yeahs!" These folks will instantly come on board for a change that they see as exciting,
beneficial, and inspiring. The second cluster, she said, is the "Yeah, buts." This group watches
and waits while the "Oh yeahs" jump on board and take the change for a test drive. After the
change proves worthy, usually once a full year has gone by, they're willing to hop up to the
wheel. Last are the "No way in hecks." This cluster holds stubbornly to the old ways. Even in
the light of success experienced by the first two groups, they will not change until forced to
change. That's where a risk-taking, forward-seeing administrator proves a wonderful ally.

Several of the contributors to this book shared that very experience in their schools.
Monck began by initiating a full flexible schedule into a library that had been fixed for 15 years.
She says that it took a lot of patience and determination to wait for the teachers to come around.

To establish credibility with a seemingly skeptical staff, I chose to immediately
begin working with a couple of energetic, innovative and cooperative teachers. I
made sure that the units and projects we worked on were very visible, and
enlisted their help in spreading the word and "talking up" what we were doing.
As word got around and other teachers saw the exciting things that were going
on in their media center, more and more teachers were willing to work with me
to provide their students with the optimum learning experience (n. pag.).

Myers had the same experience.

> When I first began collaborating, I chose teachers with whom I really connected and suggested what I could help them do....They welcomed my input and the opportunity to work with me. After others heard what I did with one teacher, they came to me and said, "Could you do with my class what you did with Mrs. M's class?" (n. pag.)

Likewise, Sherouse adds:

> I planned a unit with one teacher and when she saw the level of assistance I could offer, and the fact that I was willing to share full responsibility for the unit, the word spread. Several additional requests came in. Many of the units I helped design are still in use (n. pag.).

What are the keys then? They are several. Respect individual strengths. Form alliances with the collaborative superstars, the "Oh yeahs." Create initial successes with them. Advertise these successes. Build on them. Remain flexible. Don't expect everyone to participate at the same level. Learn to compromise for the sake of forward momentum. Remember: word of mouth is the best ally you have. Spread the word. And above all, keep the faith!

Resources

Berkowitz, Robert E. "TIPS (Teaching Information Problem-Solving): Collaboration for Success." *The Big 6 Teaching Technology & Information Skills eNewsletter*. E-1:2 (Spring 2000).

Bishop, Kay and Nancy Larimer. "Literacy through Collaboration." *Teacher Librarian* 27:1 (October 1999): 15–20.

Brown, Jill. Personal interview. 12 Feb. 2001.

Brown, Patricia Mahoney. Personal interview. 14 Feb. 2001.

Butt, Rhonda and Christine Jameson. "Steps to Collaborative Teaching."

"Collaborative Planning: How It's Done." *NEMA—Nebraska Educational Media Association.* 20 July 2000 <http://nema.k12.ne.us/CheckIt/model.html>.

Donham, Jean. "Collaboration in the Media Center: Building Partnerships for Learning." *NASSP Bulletin* 83:605 (March 1999): 20–26.

Farwell, Sybil. "Successful Models for Collaborative Planning." *Knowledge Quest* 26:2 (January/February 1998): 24–30.

Garthwait, Abigail. Personal interview. 17 Feb. 2001.

Gniewek, Debra. "Philadelphia Library Power: Collaboration Form." *Book Report* 18:2 (October 1999): 34–35.

Grover, Robert. *Collaboration*. Chicago: American Association of School Librarians, 1996.

Hand, Dorcas. Personal interview. 10 Feb. 2001.

Haycock, Ken. "Collaborative Program Planning and Teaching." *Teacher Librarian* 27:1 (October 1999): 38.

Haycock, Ken. "Fostering Collaboration, Leadership and Information Literacy: Common Behaviors of Uncommon Principals and Faculties." *NASSP Bulletin* 83:805 (March 1999): 82–87.

McIntire, Kristin. Personal interview. 12 Feb. 2001.

Monck, Deborah A. Personal interview. 11 Feb. 2001.

Muronaga, Karen and Violet Harada. "The Art of Collaboration." *Teacher Librarian* 27:1 (October 1999): 9–14.

Myers, Sue. Personal interview. 12 Feb. 2001.

Sherouse, Linda D. Personal interview. 13 Feb. 2001.

Stith, Rebecca. Personal interview. 12 Feb. 2001.

Van der Meulen, Ann. Personal interview. 16 Feb. 2001.

Van Deusen, Jean Donham and Julie I. Tallman. "The Impact of Scheduling on Curriculum Consultation and Information Skills Instruction: Part One, The 1993–94 AASL/Highsmith Research Award Study." *School Library Media Quarterly* 23:1 (Fall 1994): 17–25.

White, Karen. Personal interview. 12 Feb. 2001.

Witte-Meredith, Nancy. Personal interview. 11 Feb. 2001.

Chapter Four

Using the Template

Elements of the Template

The template used in this book was designed after poring over numerous templates from professional resources and colleagues, and examining many more from the contributors. The best elements from each source were borrowed, and then several contributors were asked to "test drive" the result. The template is both comprehensive and user-friendly. The elements are as follows:

Header: Includes Unit Title, Library Media Specialist Name and Title, Teacher Name(s) and Title, School Name, School Address, School Phone Number, and Library Media Specialist E-mail Address

Grade Level: Grade(s) that has participated in this unit.

Unit Overview: Description of the unit of study, focusing on goals, student learning, and student activity.

Time Frame: From start to finish, the time the unit takes to complete.

Content Area Standards: Exclusive of Information Skills Standards (listed on p. 25), content area(s) and standards targeted for each, drawn from local, state, or national guidelines.

Information Power Information Literacy Standards and Indicators: Drawn from IP Literacy Standards document in *Information Power: Building Partnerships for Learning.* (AASL 1998). Information Literacy Standards are reproduced with permission here. To view the indicators, AASL invites you to read *Information Power: Building Partnerships for Learning.*

Cooperative Teaching Plan: Major teaching responsibilities of the Library Media Specialist and teaching partner(s) for this unit.

Library Media Specialist Will:

Teacher(s) Will:

Resources: A list of outstanding resources for use in the unit and a summary of other helpful sources.

Print

Electronic

Audiovisuals

Equipment

Product or Culminating Activity: A description of the student activity, product, or work that makes clear student learning.

Assessment Overview: A description of the student activity, product, or work that is assessed during the unit, with notation of who assesses it and how it is assessed. Assessment tool(s) (rubric, checklist, or other) is included where available.

Adaptations and Extensions: Suggestions of other activities that might extend from this unit (such as speakers or additional products) and how the unit might be adapted to meet the needs of students who are exceptional learners, whether challenged or gifted, as well as those with varied learning styles.

Attachments: Handouts, graphic organizers, and rubrics.

INFORMATION POWER

The Nine Information Literacy Standards
for Student Learning

Excerpted with permission from Chapter 2, "Information Literacy Standards for Student Learning," of *Information Power: Building Partnerships for Learning* (AASL, 1998). For copies of the Indicators, referenced in each unit by number, see the print volume.

Information Literacy

Standard 1: The student who is information literate accesses information efficiently and effectively.

Standard 2: The student who is information literate evaluates information critically and competently.

Standard 3: The student who is information literate uses information accurately and creatively.

Independent Learning

Standard 4: The student who is an independent learner is information literate and pursues information related to personal interests.

Standard 5: The student who is an independent learner is information literate and appreciates literature and other creative expressions of information.

Standard 6: The student who is an independent learner is information literate and strives for excellence in information seeking and knowledge generation.

Social Responsibility

Standard 7: The student who contributes positively to the learning community and to society is information literate and recognizes the importance of information to a democratic society.

Standard 8: The student who contributes positively to the learning community and to society is information literate and practices ethical behavior in regard to information and information technology.

Standard 9: The student who contributes positively to the learning community and to society is information literate and participates effectively in groups to pursue and generate information.

American Association of School Librarians and Association for Educational Communication. *Information Power: Building Partnerships for Learning*. Chicago: American Library Association, 1998.

Figure 4.1 **Blank Template**

Unit Title
Library Media Specialist Name and Title
Teacher Name(s) and Title
School Name
School Address
School Phone Number
Library Media Specialist E-mail Address

Grade Level:

Unit Overview:

Time Frame:

Content Area Standards:

Information Power Information Literacy Standards and Indicators:

Cooperative Teaching Plan:

    Library Media Specialist Will:

    Teacher(s) Will:

Resources:

Product or Culminating Activity:

Assessment Overview:

Adaptations and Extensions:

Art: The Touring Company

Patricia M. Brown, School Library Media Specialist
Gustavo Glorioso, Art Teacher; Jennifer Matteson, Grade 5 Teacher
Benjamin Franklin Elementary School
500 Parkhurst Blvd., Kenmore, NY 14223
716-874-8415
pat_brown@kenton.k12.ny.us

Grade Level: 5

Unit Overview: Art: The Touring Company introduces children to art history, the basis for the study of human experience across the ages. The examination of artwork puts into perspective the cultural and social worlds in which the artists' creations arose. Using a multidisciplinary and multicultural approach, students gather, analyze, and report information on artists and artistic movements and periods. Research culminates in the publication of a biography, which is added to the school library collection, and a visual time line displayed along the school corridors.

Time Frame: One semester

Content Area Standards: New York State Learning Standards
<http://www.nysatl.nysed.gov/standards.html>

English Language Arts, Elementary

Standard 2. Language for Literary Response and Expression: Students will read and listen to oral, written, and electronically produced texts and performances from American and world literature; relate texts and performances to their own lives; and develop an understanding of the diverse social, historical, and cultural dimensions the texts and performances represent. As speakers and writers, students will use oral and written language that follows the accepted conventions of the English language for self-expression and artistic creation.
2.2 Speaking and writing for literary response involves presenting interpretations, analyses, and reactions to the content and language of a text. Speaking and writing for literary expression involves producing imaginative texts that use language and text structures that are inventive and often multilayered.
Indicator. Observe the conventions of grammar and usage, spelling, and punctuation.

Standard 3. Language for Critical Analysis and Evaluation: Students will listen, speak, read, and write for critical analysis and evaluation. As listeners and readers, students will analyze experiences, ideas, information, and issues presented by others using a variety of established criteria. As speakers and writers, they will use oral and written language that follows the accepted conventions of the English language to present, from a variety of perspectives, their opinions and judgments on experiences, ideas, information, and issues.
3.1 Listening and reading to analyze and evaluate experiences, ideas, information, and issues requires using evaluative criteria from a variety of perspectives and recognizing the difference in evaluations based on different sets of criteria.
Indicator. Monitor and adjust their own oral and written presentations to meet criteria for competent performance (e.g., in writing, the criteria might include development of position,

organization, appropriate vocabulary, mechanics, and neatness. In speaking, the criteria might include good content, effective delivery, diction, posture, poise, and eye contact).

The Arts, Elementary

Standard 3. Responding to and Analyzing Works of Art: Students will respond critically to a variety of works in the arts, connecting the individual work to other works and to other aspects of human endeavor and thought.

3.3 Visual Arts: Students will reflect on, interpret, and evaluate works of art, using the language of art criticism. Students will analyze the visual characteristics of the natural and built environment and explain the social, cultural, psychological, and environmental dimensions of the visual arts. Students will compare the ways in which a variety of ideas, themes, and concepts are expressed through the visual arts with the ways they are expressed in other disciplines.

Indicator. Explain their reflections about the meanings, purposes, and sources of works of art; describe their responses to the works and the reasons for those responses.

Indicator. Explain the visual and other sensory qualities (surfaces, colors, textures, shape, sizes, volumes) found in a wide variety of artworks.

Indicator. Explain the themes that are found in works of visual art and how the artworks are related to other forms of art (dance, music, theatre, and so on).

Standard 4. Understanding the Cultural Dimensions and Contributions of the Arts: Students will develop an understanding of the personal and cultural forces that shape artistic communication and how the arts in turn shape the diverse cultures of past and present society.

4.4 Visual Arts: Students will explore art and artifacts from various historical periods and world cultures to discover the roles that art plays in the lives of people of a given time and place and to understand how the time and place influence visual characteristics of the artwork. Students will explore art to understand the social, cultural, and environmental dimensions of human society.

Indicator. Look at and discuss a variety of artworks and artifacts from world cultures to discover some important ideas, issues, and events of those cultures.

Indicator. Look at a variety of artworks and artifacts from diverse cultures of the United States and identify some distinguishing characteristics.

Social Studies, Elementary

Standard 2. World History: Students will use a variety of intellectual skills to demonstrate their understanding of major ideas, eras, themes, developments, and turning points in world history and examine the broad sweep of history from a variety of perspectives.

2.2 Establishing timeframes, exploring different periodizations, examining themes across time and within cultures, and focusing on how important turning points in world history help organize the study of world cultures and civilizations.

Indicator. Develop time lines that display important events and eras from world history.

2.3 Study of the major social, political, cultural, and religious developments in world history involves learning about the important roles and contributions of individuals and groups.

Indicator. Understand the roles and contributions of individuals and groups to social, political, economic, cultural, scientific, technological, and religious practices and activities.

Indicator. Gather and present information about important developments from world history.

2.4 The skills of historical analysis include the ability to investigate differing and competing interpretations of the theories of history, hypothesize about why interpretations change over time, explain the importance of historical evidence, and understand the concepts of change and continuity over time.

Indicator. View historic events through the eyes of those who were there, as shown in their art, writings, music, and artifacts.

Information Power Information Literacy Standards and Indicators: 1.1, 1.2, 1.4, 1.5, 2.1, 2.2, 2.3, 2.4, 3.1, 3.2, 3.3, 3.4, 5.2, 5.3, 6.1, 6.2, 7.1, 7.2, 8.1, 8.2, 8.3, 9.1, 9.2, 9.3, 9.4.

Cooperative Teaching Plan:

Library Media Specialist Will:

- Meet biweekly with classroom and art teacher to discuss and monitor progress of project.
- Review techniques of searching the Internet with students.
- Discuss the importance of evaluation of print and nonprint information with students.
- Assist students in using the library media center for research.
- Coordinate development of visual and written timeline: portrait of the artist, historical events and scientific developments during the artist's life, two pieces of the artist's work.
- Guide students' research strategies in compiling information from a variety of resources.
- Add completed student biographies of the artists to the library collection for circulation.

Fifth Grade Teacher Will:

- Guide students in English Language Arts to read and write analytically and cogently by:
  - Gathering and interpreting information from appropriate forms of various media, using strategies for note taking and synthesizing material;
  - Presenting material clearly and concisely;
  - Using techniques for producing prose though drafting, revising, and proofreading;
  - Employing the conventions of good writing, e.g., correct spelling, punctuation, capitalization, well-constructed sentences and paragraphs;
  - Learning critical criteria for evaluation of information, ideas, and issues.

- Guide students in their Social Studies activities by:
  - Presenting an overview of major idea, eras, themes, developments and turning points in history as they pertain to art and its development;
  - Assisting students in using critical thinking skills as they pertain to an investigation of the historical record.

Art Teacher Will:

- Survey artistic development from earliest expression in cave paintings through modern movements such as Impressionism, Realism, Cubism, and Surrealism to current trends.
- Discuss art production and criticism as they contribute to the understanding of artists.
- Lead students to evaluate art with criteria: to differentiate between preference and judgment, to respect differences of opinion about art, to appreciate the value of art, to express individual opinions effectively, and to value their own and others' responses.
- Assist each student in selecting a particular artist to study in detail and to produce a one-volume illustrated biography to be added to the school library.
- Guide students in the illustration of their reports and of their individual portions of a timeline to be displayed in the school corridors.

Resources:

Print

Art for Young People series. New York: Sterling Publishing Co.

Art in History series. Des Plaines, Illinois: Heinemann Interactive Library.

Art Revolutions series. New York: Peter Bedrick Books.

Batterberry, Ariane Ruskin. *Pantheon Study of American Art for Young People*. New York: Pantheon Books, 1976.

Beckett, Wendy. *Sister Wendy's 1000 Masterpieces*. New York: DK Publishers, 1999.

Gardner, Helen. *Gardner's Art Through the Ages*, 10th ed. Fort Worth: Harcourt Brace, 1996.

Getting to Know the World's Greatest Artists series. New York: Children's Press.

Glubok, Shirley. *Painting*. Great Lives Series. New York: Scribner's Sons, 1994.

Ingpen, Robert W. *Art and Technology Through the Ages*. Illustrated by Robert Ingpen, text by Philip Wilkinson and Jacqueline Dineen. New York: Chelsea House, 1994.

Janson, H.W. *History of Art for Young People*. 5th ed. New York: H.H. Abrams, 1997.

Lauber, Patricia. *Painters of the Caves*. Washington, D.C.: National Geographic Society, 1998.

Electronic

"All about Art." *ThinkQuest*. 21 July 2001
    <http://library.thinkquest.org/J001159/?tqskip=1>.

"Artists." *Netscape*. 21 July 2001
    <http://search.netscape.com/browse.psp?cp=nrpussmm&id=447500>.

Primary Search Online. EBSCO Publishing. (Requires subscription)

"Renaissance Artists." *The Masters*. 21 July 2001
    <http://www.geocities.com/Paris/Gallery/2892/renaissance.html>.

Audiovisuals

Art of the Western World. Nine videocassettes, Santa Barbara: (Intellimation), 1989.

How to Visit an Art Museum. Videocassette. Tellens, 1993.

The Louvre. Videocassette. Monterey, California: Monterey Home Video, 1978.

Product or Culminating Activity: Individual illustrated biographies of artists studied are placed in the library circulating collection. The visual time line from the earliest art to contemporary art depicts a complete historical panorama of art history and related cultural manifestations. The time line is on display during the annual school art show for parents as well as students to enjoy.

Assessment Overview: The entire teaching team involved evaluates the completed biographies and considers as criteria the fullness and accuracy of research, the quality of writing, and the creativeness of the accompanying illustrations.

Figure 4.2 **Art: The Touring Company**

Biographical Worksheet

Room No. _____

Name: _____

Full Name of Artist: _____

Date of Birth: _____ Date of Death: _____

Place of Birth: _____

Interesting Events During Artist's Childhood:

_____

_____

_____

_____

Schooling:

_____

_____

_____

_____

People Who Influenced the Artist's Work:

_____

_____

_____

_____

Figure 4.2   (continued from page 31)

Influence of the Artist on Others:

_____

_____

_____

_____

Period of Art Represented:

_____

_____

_____

_____

Major Artistic Works (indicate name of work, date of work, and museum that has the original):

_____

_____

_____

_____

Critical Opinions About the Artist's Work:

_____

_____

_____

_____

Further Interesting Facts:

_____

_____

_____

_____

Figure 4.3   **Art: The Touring Company**

Time Line Worksheet

Name: _____   Room No. _____

Full Name of Artist: _____

Date of Birth: _____   Date of Death: _____

On separate paper, please complete the following:

1. From world history, choose a major event that occurred during your artist's lifetime and write a paragraph of 6 to 10 sentences about it. Illustrate the event.

2. From United States history (or the history of the Americas), choose a major event that occurred during your artist's lifetime and write a paragraph of 6 to 10 sentences about it. Illustrate the event.

3. From science or technology, choose a major scientific or technological discovery or achievement that occurred during your artist's lifetime and write a paragraph of 6 to 10 sentences about it. Illustrate the discovery/achievement.

4. Illustrate two major works of your artist and write a paragraph of 6 to 10 sentences describing your response to and interpretation of each.

5. Draw a portrait of your artist.

Figure 4.4   **Art: The Touring Company**

Research Checklist

Name: _____   Room No. _____

Full Name of Artist: _____

Did I …

❑ 1.   Check the OPAC?

❑ 2.   Examine general encyclopedias?

❑ 3.   Examine art encyclopedias and reference works?

❑ 4.   Search the Internet?

❑ 5.   Use electronic reference sources (CD-ROMs, videocassettes)?

❑ 6.   Continue research at the public library?

❑ 7.   Consult with the Library Media Specialist on the progress of my study?

❑ 8.   Compile a bibliography of all resources in MLA format?

Figure 4.5 **Art: The Touring Company**

Evaluation of Research Biography

Room No. _____

Name: _____

Evaluator(s): _____

_____

Evaluative Criteria	Excellent	Good	Fair	Poor
Used library resources effectively.				
Demonstrated ability to search for information online.				
Incorporated a variety of print and nonprint materials in research.				
Performed research independently.				
Demonstrated comprehension of materials.				
Synthesized materials creatively.				
Organized materials effectively.				
Exhibited conventions of good writing.				
Included accurate information.				
Cited sources correctly (MLA).				
Understood relation of artist to world history, science/technology, and art history.				
Combined text and illustrations in an appealing graphic format.				

Student's Final Grade: _____

Grade Level: 4

Unit Overview: Biography Bash: A Study of Heroes teaches critical thinking, research process, and biographical research, as well as creative presentation skills. It begins, over the first half of the year, with a study of the qualities of heroism using a list of heroic traits through literature and history. Students then choose a person who reflects heroic qualities to study in depth. During a field trip to the public library, students begin individual research, which continues back in the library media center, culminating in an individual book about each hero and a wax museum.

Time Frame: 8 to 9 weeks

Content Area Standards: Texas Essential Knowledge and Skills (TEKS)
    <http://www.tea.state.tx.us/teks/>

English Language Arts and Reading, Grade 4

Standard 5. Listening/speaking/audiences: The student speaks clearly and appropriately to different audiences for different purposes and occasions.

5.A adapt spoken language such as word choice, diction, and usage to the audience, purpose, and occasion.

Standard 8. Reading/variety of texts: The student reads widely for different purposes in varied sources.

8.B select varied sources such as nonfiction, novels, textbooks, newspapers, and magazines when reading for information or pleasure.

Standard 15. Writing/purposes: The student writes for a variety of audiences and purposes, and in a variety of forms.

15.A write to express, discover, record, develop, reflect on ideas, and to problem solve;

15.C write to inform such as to explain, describe, report, and narrate;

15.E exhibit an identifiable voice in personal narratives and in stories.

Standard 19. Writing/writing processes: The student selects and uses writing processes for self-initiated and assigned writing.

15.H proofread his/her own writing and that of others;

15.I select and use reference materials and resources as needed for writing, revising, and editing final drafts.

Social Studies, Grade 4

Standard 4.22. Social studies skills: The student applies critical-thinking skills to organize and use information acquired from a variety of sources including electronic technology.

4.22.A differentiate between, locate, and use primary and secondary sources such as computer software; interviews; biographies; oral, print, and visual material; and artifacts to acquire information about the United States and Texas;

4.22.B analyze information by sequencing, categorizing, identifying cause-and-effect relationships, comparing, contrasting, find the main idea, summarizing, making generalizations and predictions, and drawing inferences and conclusions.

Standard 5.23. Social studies skills: The student communicates in written, oral, and visual forms.

5.23.D create written and visual material such as journal entries, reports, graphic organizers, outlines, and bibliographies;

5.23.E use standard grammar, spelling, sentence structure, and punctuation.

Social Studies, Grade 5

Standard 5.5. History: The student understands important issues, events, and individuals of the 20th century in the United States.

5.5.B identify the accomplishments of notable individuals such as Carrie Chapman Catt, Dwight Eisenhower, Martin Luther King, Jr., Rosa Parks, Colin Powell, and Franklin D. Roosevelt who have made contributions to society in the areas of civil rights. women's rights, military actions, and politics.

Information Power Information Literacy Standards and Indicators: 1.1, 1.2, 1.3, 1.4, 1.5, 2.1, 2.2, 2.3, 2.4, 3.1, 3.2, 3.3, 3.4, 4.2, 5.3, 6.2, 8.2. 8.3

Cooperative Teaching Plan:

Librarian Will:
- Meet with the teachers to refine unit and plan for changes.
- Revise the instructions for the students.
- Introduce online sources in the Computer Lab, including Gale Biography Resource Online Database and the "Biography" page at InfoPlease for help in choosing a topic.
- Arrange the trip to Montrose Branch Library.
- Lead trip to the library and provide orientation to branch library during the visit.
- Work with students in the adult stacks to find appropriate materials.
- Supervise individual students in locating periodicals by using indices.
- Continue to guide student research in the library media center.

Teachers Will:
- Participate in the unit revision and planning process.
- Implement the advance preparation:
  - *Character Education:* teach heroic qualities. The person studied should be a person to be admired, a person from whom the student can learn positive lessons.
  - *Teach IIM* (Independent Investigative Method) of note taking. (For children in their early research experiences, IIM offers a visual method for children to keep up with the various threads of learning.)
  - *Reading Class:* Teach students how to read a biographical piece.
  - *Study Skills:* Teach students how to extract the needed information from a biographical piece.

(By using a newspaper on Texas history and a biography of Sam Houston, we tie the skill to other curriculum topics.)

- *Study Skills:* Teach students what they need to know about each resource and how to use NoodleBib <http://www.noodletools.com/noodlebib/>.

■ Accompany students to the public library and work with them as needed in the children's area to locate juvenile biographies of their heroes.

■ Provide class time for writing and organizing. Only research may be done at home.

■ Provide computer class time to type project or continue research online as appropriate.

■ Provide time and adult support in computer class to use NoodleBib <http://www.noodletools.com/noodlebib/> to complete the bibliography.

■ Plan and schedule the wax museum.

Academic Support Coordinator will:

■ As part of the fourth grade Study Skills class, teach bibliography construction using NoodleBib <http://www.noodletools.com/noodlebib/>.

■ Reinforce IIM (Independent Investigative Method) note taking.

■ Introduce the process of researching a biography.

Resources:

Print
A broad collection of biographies written at a fourth grade reading level.

Biography Today Annual. Detroit: Gale Research, 1993–.

Current Biography series. New York: H.W. Wilson, 1940–.

Junior Book of Authors and Illustrators series. New York: H.W. Wilson, 1934–.

Osborn, Kevin. *Scholastic Encyclopedia of Sports in the United States.* New York: Scholastic, 1997.

Something About the Author series. Detroit: Gale Research, 1971–.

World Book Encyclopedia. Chicago, World Book, Inc., 2001.

Electronic
Abilock, Damon and Debbie. "NoodleBib." *NoodleTools.* 10 July 2001
    <http://www.noodletools.com/noodlebib/index.php>.

"Biographical Dictionary." *S9.com.* 21 July 2001 <http://www.s9.com/biography/>.

"Biography." *InfoPlease.* 18 July 2001 <http://www.infoplease.com/people.html>.

Biography Resource Center. 19 July 2001
    <http://www.galegroup.com/BiographyRC/about.htm>. Subscription required.

Biography.com. 21 July 2001 <http://www.biography.com/>.

Lanxner, Kenneth P. Lives, *The Biographical Resource.* 1 July 2001. 21 July 2001
    <http://amillionlives.com/>.

Product or Culminating Activity: Book with required configuration of pages that demonstrates student assimilation of information. Wax Museum oral presentation for parents and other classes.

Assessment Overview: Teacher grades each piece of the project separately using a read and respond method but no rubrics; all students are given ample time to achieve a high standard.

| Figure 4.6 | **Biography Bash: A Study of Heroes** |

Overview

Choosing a Hero: Select a personality you would like to study. The person can be living or dead, but may not be a current sports figure or movie star. You must look up at least five different people who interest you, to see if there is information available. Do not choose a topic about whom there is no information.

You will be asked to write a preliminary paragraph about your choice explaining why this person interests you and what heroic characteristics you think he or she demonstrates. These people should exhibit heroic characteristics and be people you can admire. You might even want to select a person who has, or had, the same birthday as you do! You will be making a memory book about this person's life.

Fact Web: Use your new Mind Map skills to create a visual map of your notes about this person's life. Remember, the Mind Map is a graphic representation of events in the life of your famous person. It will help you to organize his or her life before you write some of the larger pieces. Major threads might include Early Life, Family, Career, Travels, and others. This web will help you construct all the pages of your memory book, but will not be part of the final draft.

Page 1: Hero Card

Design a Hero Card, like a baseball card, for your person. The front will have a portrait of his/her face. The back will list basic facts in a format provided by your teacher.

Page 2: Map and Map Label

Complete a Map Label page provided by your teacher listing your person's name, main heroic quality or reason for importance, birth and death dates, the place in the world you think most important to the person's life and why it is so important, and your name. You will also print a map from the Internet to locate the place.

These labels will surround a world map in the hall and be connected to the correct world location by yarn. You will be expected to string the yarn from your label to the correct place on the map.

Page 3: Life Map

On a sheet of unlined copy paper, draw a path that leads through the major events in your person's life. Your life map must begin with your person's birth, and include at least seven more dates and seven other descriptive illustrations.

Page 4: Journal Entries

Become your person. Write at least two journal entries as your person would have written them.

Page 5: Letters

Become your person again. Write at least two letters (one friendly and one business) to another person in your time. In your friendly letter, describe your personal accomplishments or some hardship you may have experienced. Your business letter could set up a meeting or some other happening, or be a complaint about a problem.

Figure 4.6   (continued from page 40)

Page 6: Autobiography

Write an autobiography of your person's life. Do not reveal the identity of your person. Questions that will help you prepare this sketch are:

1. When/where did you live?
2. What are you famous for? What were some problems you had, and how did you solve them?
3. What kind of clothes do you wear?
4. What was going on in the city/state/country when you were alive?
5. Describe your family. How big is/was it? Mention your parents, siblings, spouse, and children.
6. Who were your friends?
7. List one influential person in your life, and explain why he/she was so important to you.
8. *How did you affect the lives of other people?
9. *How is life different now because of you?

   You MUST include the answer to at least one of these two questions.

Your autobiography MUST be typed.

Page 7: Hero Skills Award

Thinking of the Academy Awards as your model, invent an award to present to your person. This award should have a title that reflects the hero skills this person demonstrated most completely throughout his/her life. You should write a brief explanation of the award and why your person has won it, and draw a picture of the award.

   Also compose a guest list of three to five people who should be invited to the Awards Ceremony. These people can be alive or dead, from the time of the person or from another time, but you must explain why they should be invited. Did the invitee have a strong influence on your person, or did your person have a strong influence on the invitee? Examples include family members, friends, a scientist who depends on the discoveries of your person, and a writer who looks to your person as a teacher. Your teacher will help you with this in class.

Page 8: Birthday Party Invitation

Make an invitation to a birthday party for your personality. Decide on a theme and make it relevant to the life, career, and times in which he/she lived. Include where, when, and who is hosting the party (parents, a friend, a political party, a sports team, and so on).

Page 9: Bibliography

We will give you an appropriate form. You need to tell us exactly where you found your information. Remember to use your IIM ((Independent Investigative Method) skills.

Heroes Wax Museum Day: You will dress like your person and recite your autobiographical paragraph for an audience of students from other grades.

Figure 4.7   **Biography Bash: A Study of Heroes**

Time Line

Student: _____   Class: _____

Topic: _____

Deadline: _____

GUIDELINE DUE DATES

Cover   _____

Fact web   _____

Page 1: Hero card   _____

Page 2: Map and map label   _____

Page 3: Life map   _____

Page 4: Journal entries   _____

Page 5: Letters   _____

Page 6: Autobiography—TYPED!   _____

Page 7: Hero Skills Award   _____

Page 8: Birthday party invitation   _____

Page 9: Bibliography   _____

* You must use at least three sources, and no more than one basic encyclopedia.
* If you use the Internet, please include the date of your search in the citation.
* Only one of the three basic sources may be from the Internet.
* If you use more than three sources, you may use more than one from the Internet.

Heroes Wax Museum Day   _____

Your teacher will show you models for each page. Please do not work ahead but do stay aware of the due dates. Remember your IIM ((Independent Investigative Method) research skills.

Figure 4.8   **Biography Bash: A Study of Heroes**

Reasons for My Topic Choice

Student: _____   Class: _____

Topic: _____

Note: You must include at least one hero trait.

I decided to research _____

because:

_____

_____

_____

_____

_____

_____

Here are some questions to guide my research:

_____

_____

_____

_____

_____

_____

_____

_____

Figure 4.9   **Biography Bash: A Study of Heroes**

Autobiography

This important assignment will be typed.

This is your opportunity to show that you are an expert on your hero. You will even become your person when you share the essay aloud at the Birthday Bash Wax Museum later this month. When read aloud, your essay should be about two minutes long.

Please begin with: "I was born on (date) in (place). Then you will include important facts about your person, such as 1) What makes them interesting? Use your notes. 2) What was going on when he/she was alive? (Question 4) 3) Notice that your essay must include either Question 8 or 9. 4) You may consider answering these questions: Why did I choose this person? or Why is he/she famous? Please end with: "Did you guess who I am? I am (name of person)."

Wax Museum

We will rehearse speeches for the Birthday Bash Wax Museum in class, and you should practice your speech at home also. You will come to class the day of the Wax Museum dressed as your character. It is not too soon to begin thinking about your costume!

Hero Skills Award

Thinking of the Academy Awards as your model, invent an award to present to your person. This award should have a title that reflects the hero skills this person demonstrated most completely throughout his/her life. You should write a brief explanation of the award and why your person has won it, and draw a picture of the award.

Now compose a guest list of three to five people who should be invited to the Awards Ceremony. These people can be alive or dead, from the time of the person or from another time, but you must explain why they should be invited. Did the invitee have a strong influence on your person, or did your person have a strong influence on the invitee? Examples include family members, friends, a scientist who depends on the discoveries of your person, and a writer who looks to your person as a teacher.

Notice that the assignment has three parts:

- a description of the award;
- an illustration of the award;
- a guest list with brief explanations of why each person was invited to the celebration.

Consider your person's hero traits and contributions to the world as you create his/her own unique award. Questions to ask yourself:

- What hero trait did your person have?
- How did he/she affect the world?

Canyons by Gary Paulsen:
An Archaeological Study

Bernie Tomasso, Library Media Specialist
Cathy Wood, Grade 6 Social Studies Teacher
Leslie B. Lehn Middle School
30 Maple Ave. Port Byron NY 13140-9647
(315) 776-8939
btomasso@twcny.rr.com

Grade Level: 6

Unit Overview: *Canyons* by Gary Paulsen: An Archaeological Study introduces archaeology to sixth graders who spend a year studying various world cultures, with an emphasis on ancient and medieval civilizations. Students read the novel and complete activities related to archaeological themes and Southwest United States. In addition, students explore what constitutes a civilization and what leads to its downfall. This first research project sets the stage for five research projects completed in the sixth grade and for the research process used in subsequent years.

Time Frame: 15–20 class periods

Content Area Standards: New York State Learning Standards
<http://www.emsc.nysed.gov/top/learning.html>

Social Studies, Intermediate

Standard 1: History of the United States and New York. Students will use a variety of intellectual skills to demonstrate their understanding of major ideas, eras, themes, developments, and turning points in the history of the United States and New York.
Indicator. Understand the relationship between the relative importance of United States domestic and foreign policies over time.
Indicator. Complete well-documented and historically accurate case studies about individuals and groups who represent different ethnic, national, and religious, groups, including Native American Indians, in New York State and the United States at different times and in different locations.
Indicator. Gather and organize information about the important achievements and contributions of individuals and groups living in New York State and the United States.
Indicator. Classify major developments into categories such as social, political, economic, geographic, technological, scientific, cultural, or religious.

Standard 3: Geography. Students will use a variety of intellectual skills to demonstrate their understanding of the geography of the interdependent world in which we live—local, national, and global—including the distribution of people, places, and environments over the Earth's surface.
Indicator. Map information about people, places, and environments.
Indicator. Describe the relationships between people and environments and the connections between people and places.

Math, Science, and Technology, Intermediate

Standard 2. Students will access, generate, process, and transfer information using appropriate technologies.

Indicator. Use a variety of equipment and software packages to enter, process, display, and communicate information in different forms using text, tables, pictures, and sound.

Indicator. Access needed information from printed media, electronic databases, and community resources.

Indicator. Demonstrate ability to evaluate information.

English Language Arts, Intermediate

Standard 1. Students will read, write, listen, and speak for information and understanding.

Indicator. Interpret and analyze information from textbooks and nonfiction books for young adults, as well as reference materials, audio and media presentations, oral interviews, graphs, charts, diagrams, and electronic databases intended for a general audience.

Indicator. Compare and synthesize information from different sources.

Indicator. Use a wide variety of strategies for selecting, organizing, and categorizing information.

Indicator. Relate new information to prior knowledge and experience.

Indicator. Produce oral and written reports on topics related to all school subjects.

Indicator. Establish an authoritative stance on the subject and provide references to establish the validity and verifiability of the information presented.

Indicator. Use the process of pre-writing, drafting, revising, and proofreading ("the writing process") to produce well-constructed informational texts.

Indicator. Use standard English for formal presentation of information and vocabulary, selecting appropriate grammatical constructions and vocabulary, using a variety of sentence structures, and observing the rules of punctuation, capitalization, and spelling.

Standard 2. Students will read, write, listen, and speak for literary response and expression.

Indicator. Recognize different levels of meaning.

Indicator. Present responses to and interpretations of literature, making references to the literary elements found in the text and connections with their personal knowledge and experience.

Indicator. Use standard English effectively.

Standard 3. Students will read, write, listen, and speak for critical analysis and evaluation.

Indicator. Evaluate their own and others' work based on a variety of criteria (e.g., logic, clarity, comprehensiveness, conciseness, originality, conventionality) and recognize the varying effectiveness of different approaches.

Information Power Information Literacy Standards and Indicators: 1.4, 1.5, 2.1, 2.3, 2.4, 3.1, 3.3, 3.4, 5.3

Cooperative Teaching Plan:

Library Media Specialist Will:

■ Provide background materials on archaeology and Texas for the classroom.

■ Cooperatively develop culminating activities.

■ Discuss dynamics of group work using "Finding Good Teammates" handout.

- Discuss choosing a topic that will interest the student and also be at an appropriate level of difficulty using "Preparing an Exhibition" handout.
- Provide overview of topics and time line for completion of project using "Canyon Projects Overview" handout.
- Provide bibliographic instruction.
- Provide feedback on project according to previous discussion on what constitutes an exemplary project, referring to "Preparing an Exhibition" handout as a guideline.

Classroom Teacher Will:
- Cooperatively develop culminating activities.
- Introduce unit and social studies vocabulary on archaeology.
- Conduct "Archaeological Dig" activity.
- Read *Canyons* with students.
- Discuss novel and assign journal activities. (Journal Activity: Each time that we read *Canyons*, you are to record your thoughts and feelings about what you've just read. They do not have to be in complete sentences—words or phrases are fine—but they must show that you are becoming involved in the story.)
- Provide examples of projects while reading the novel so students have an awareness of culminating activities.
- Grade oral presentations and project.

Resources:

Print
Heinrich, Ann. *America the Beautiful: Texas*. Chicago: Childrens Press, 1999.

Paulsen, Gary. *Canyons*. New York: Laurel Leaf, 1991.

Travel brochures and maps available from Texas Department of Transportation 1-800-452-9292 and El Paso Convention & Visitors Bureau 1-800-351-6024.

World Book Encyclopedia. Chicago: World Book, Inc., 2001.

Electronic
Carlisle, Jeffrey D. "Apache Indians." *Handbook of Texas Online*. 15 Feb. 1999. 9 July 2001 <http://www.tsha.utcxas.cdu/handbook/online/articles/view/AA/bma33.html>.

The City of El Paso, Texas. 2001. 9 July 2001 <http://www.ci.el-paso.tx.us/>.

"Gary Paulsen." *Books@Random*. 2001. 9 July 2001 <http://www.randomhouse.com/features/garypaulsen/>.

"The Plains Indians of Texas." *El Centro College History Department*. 9 July 2001 <http://www.angelfire.com/tx2/ecc/plains.html>.

Texas Online. 2001. 4 May 2001. 9 July 2001 <http://www.state.tx.us/>.

TravelTex. 9 July 2001 <http://www.traveltex.com/start.asp?SN=707959>.

Product or Culminating Activity: Oral presentations and a selected product.

Assessment Overview: Teacher and peer assessment of products using teacher-developed rubric. Self-assessment and teacher assessment of oral presentations using Oral Presentation Rubric. Library Media Specialist provides oral critique of oral presentation graphic based on previous discussion of traits of an exemplary project and the "Preparing an Exhibition" handout.

Figure 4.10 *Canyons* **by Gary Paulsen: An Archaeological Study**

Project Overview

Students may work with a partner with teacher permission. Please be aware that you will share the same grade. Both partners must demonstrate their participation in the project.

Topics may be chosen from the following list:

1. Create a newspaper using historical events referred to in the novel *Canyons* by Gary Paulsen. This will require research about the time period between 1860 and 1890.

2. Research and develop a time line that shows changes between the 1800s and the present. Research changes in technology, military weapons, life styles of Apache Indians, and so on.

3. Research and develop a time line of other events that occurred between 1860 and 1890. You may choose United States or world events, or a special topic, such as sports or technology.

4. Build a learning center about the book *Canyons*. Your center will look like a science fair display board with information about the author, characters, setting, plot, and so on.

5. Conduct a research project about the Apache Indians. This will include information about their culture, history, beliefs, traditions, government, folktales, and present day life.

6. Research American soldiers in the 1800s. This will include finding information about their duties, uniforms, weapons, training, life in a fort, and so on.

7. Write two one-page letters to the editor. First, express your support of the military action at Dog Canyon. Then, oppose the military action at Dog Canyon. Include facts from the book.

8. Prepare a storyboard. Include characters, setting, plot, author, and themes.

9. Develop and perform a skit showing one or more important scenes approved by the teacher.

10. Conduct an author study including information about Paulsen and other works he has written.

11. Report on desert life. Include desert plants as well as animals that live in the desert.

12. Prepare a music report. Research what a symphony or other piece of classical music includes. Locate a recording of Mahler's *Resurrection Symphony* or an example of similar classical music from the same period. Write a report about the composer. Include details about the piece and why the composer chose to name it as he or she did.

13. Undertake a geography project. Draw and provide a legend for a map, which includes the El Paso, Texas, area, the natural resources that are found there, and manufactured products. Describe the climate of the area also.

Finding Good Teammates

Your can save yourself much trouble in a team project by being careful when forming teams. Please find teammates who are compatible with you in the following areas:

- **Schedule:** If you can't find time when the whole team can meet, you will be miserable.

- **Interests:** If you can't get all teammates interested in the same topics, you won't build a quality piece.

- **Attitudes:** If all of you want to be the boss, you'll eat each other alive.

- **Work Habits:** If highly organized people try to work with "whenever" people, everyone goes nuts.

- **Goals for This Course:** If you want to take a C and run, don't team up with perfectionists.

Final Note: It is better to have a mix of talents on your team than for all teammates to have similar strengths and weaknesses.

Guidelines For Preparing an Exhibition

1. In an exhibition, you are asked to demonstrate:

   - **Knowledge**
     What you know and what you've learned.

   - **Skills**
     How you communicate your knowledge to others.
     How you work with others.

2. In an exhibition, you must make sure:

   - To clearly state your major ideas. Say simply and directly what a person should learn from your exhibit.

   - To use examples to fully develop your ideas. Once you've decided what you're saying, then give examples to prove it.

   - To check your exhibit for grammar, spelling, and neatness. Take pride in your work; it says who you are.

   - To include graphic illustrations that provide information about your exhibit. Create visuals that help people understand your major ideas.

   - To check your exhibit for accuracy of information. Make sure you have the facts to support your ideas.

3. In a cooperative exhibition, make sure that everyone knows what is expected of him or her, that the work is evenly divided, and that a schedule is developed to complete the task.

Figure 4.13   *Canyons* **by Gary Paulsen: An Archaeological Study**

Archaeological Dig Notes

Leader _____

Scribe _____

Artist _____

Presenter _____

What type of society lived at your site:

❑ Hunters and Gatherers?   ❑ Fishermen?

❑ Farmers and Herders?   ❑ Traders?

List evidence of economic activity.

List evidence of culture or social structure.

Scribe: Describe artifacts here.	**Artist:** Describe artifacts here.
1.	1.
2.	2.
3.	3.
4.	4.

Presenter Notes:

Figure 4.14 *Canyons by Gary Paulsen: An Archaeological Study*

Self Assessment Criteria and Teacher Scoring Guide

Completeness

■ Have you completed all task requirements?

Clarity

■ Does your exhibition demonstrate a logical and understandable plan of organization?
■ Are your major ideas clearly stated?
■ Are your major ideas fully developed through the use of appropriate examples?
■ Has attention been given to grammar, spelling, and neatness?

Research and Information

■ Is your information accurate and relevant?
■ Does it cover the basic facts and important concepts?
■ Have you included appropriate documentation?
■ Have you used reliable and varied sources?

Graphic Representation

■ Are your graphic illustrations useful rather than merely decorative?
■ Do your graphics provide information about your exhibition?
■ Do your graphics help people understand your major ideas?

Student Reflection

■ What did you learn?
■ What did your class learn?
■ What skills did you learn or improve upon?
■ What did you do well?
■ What would you have done differently?

Teacher Scoring Guide

Quality	Possible Points	Score
a. Project is done on time	20 pts.	_____
b. Project is neat and in an acceptable form	20 pts.	_____
c. Project shows an understanding of the book	20 pts.	_____
d. Project shows understanding of the assignment	20 pts.	_____
e. Project shows effort	20 pts.	_____
	Total	_____

Figure 4.15 *Canyons* **by Gary Paulsen: An Archaeological Study**

Oral Presentation Rubric

EXEMPLARY	SATISFACTORY	NOT YET
The talk reflects a thorough understanding of the project and relates it to *Canyons*.	The talk reflects a good understanding of the project and relates it to *Canyons*.	The talk reflects little understanding of the project and is unrelated to *Canyons*.
Audience questions are answered thoroughly and accurately.	Audience questions are answered, but leave some ambiguity or need for clarification.	Audience questions are not all addressed or are confusing. Leaves audience with too many questions.
The talk is well prepared as evidenced through a smooth performance.	The talk is prepared but not completely smooth. Speaker depends too much on notes or notes are unorganized.	The talk is not well prepared or smooth. Speaker is obviously lacking notes and/or information.
Voice level and eye contact are appropriate.	Voice level is low and/or little eye contact with audience. Talks too slowly or quickly.	Voice level is too low. No eye contact with audience.

Carnival of Animals

Nancy Witte-Meredith, Library Media Specialist

Teachers: Joan Davis, Physical Education; Carol Goff, Art; Linda Hoidalen, Music

R.D. Seymour School

185 Hartford Avenue, East Granby, CT 04026

860-653-7214

mwitmere@aol.com

Grade Level: 5

Unit Overview: In Carnival of Animals, students experience the integrated disciplines of music, art, literature, and dance through Saint-Saëns' composition, *Carnival of the Animals*, a collection of short orchestral pieces illustrating the Romantic Period concept of program music. In the library media center, students encounter Ogden Nash's interpretation of *Carnival of the Animals* and acquire an animal to research and portray. In cooperative learning groups, students build on research and pursue expressions in art, music, and physical education classes, culminating in a public performance that employs student-created dances, costumes, scenery, and programs.

Time Frame: 16 weeks

Content Area Standards: The Connecticut Framework K–12 Curricular Goals and Standards
<http://www.state.ct.us/sde/dtl/curriculum/index.htm>

The Arts: Dance, Grades 5–8

Content Standard 1: Elements and Style. Students will identify and perform elements and dance skills.
Performance Standard. Demonstrate the following movement skills and explain the underlying principles: alignment, balance, initiation of movement, articulation of isolated body parts, weight shift, elevation and landing.
Performance Standard. Transfer a rhythmic pattern from sound to movement.
Performance Standard. Memorize and reproduce movement sequences and dances.
Content Standard 2: Choreography. Students will understand choreographic principles, processes and structure.
Performance Standard. Demonstrate the ability to work cooperatively in pairs and small groups during the choreographic process.
Content Standard 3: Meaning. Students will understand how dance creates and communicates meaning.
Performance Standard. Demonstrate and/or explain how lighting and costuming can contribute to the meaning of a dance.

The Arts: Music, Grades 5–8

Content Standard 6: Analysis. Students will listen to, describe and analyze music.
Performance Standard. Demonstrate knowledge of the basic principles of meter, rhythm, tonality, intervals, chords and harmonic progressions in their analyses of music.
Content Standard 8: Connections. Students will make connections between music, other disciplines and daily life.

Performance Standard. Compare in two or more arts how the characteristic materials of each art (sound in music, visual stimuli in visual arts, movement in dance, human relationships in theatre) can be used to transform similar events, scenes, emotions or ideas into works of art.
Performance Standard. Describe the ways in which the principles and subject matter of music and other disciplines taught in the school are interrelated.

The Arts, Visual Arts, Grades 5–8

Content Standard 1: Media. Students will understand, select and apply media, techniques and processes.
Performance Standard. Select media, techniques and processes to communicate ideas, reflect on their choices and analyze what makes them effective.
Content Standard 2: Elements and Principles. Students will understand and apply elements and organizational principles of art.
Performance Standard. Select and use the elements of art and principles of design to improve communication of their ideas.
Content Standard 6: Connections. Students will make connections between the visual arts, other disciplines and daily life.
Performance Standard. Describe ways in which the principles and subject matter of the visual arts and other disciplines taught in school are interrelated.

Information Power Information Literacy Standards and Indicators: 1.1, 1.4, 1.5, 2.2, 2.4, 3.1, 3.2, 3.3, 3.4, 5.2, 9.1, 9.2, 9.3

Cooperative Teaching Plan:

Library Media Specialist Will:
- Introduce students to the unit and assign students to cooperative learning groups, which will remain consistent throughout the unit (with all teachers).
- Review the research process for this project and assign each group an animal.
- Read rough drafts of animal reports.
- Introduce the Animal Research Project Checklists and conference with groups to suggest revisions based on their responses and rough drafts.
- Assess student animal research reports based on stated guidelines in the checklists.
- Introduce students to Ogden Nash and his poetry based on *Carnival of the Animals*.
- Select student narrators to read the poetry at the performance and coach in rehearsals.
- Participate as part of the teaching team during the rehearsals and final performance.

Art Teacher Will:
- Review multiview sketching with the students.
- Assess the student-created 4" × 6" animal sketches based on the stated guidelines.
- Teach and implement the block cutting process using completed animal sketches.
- Teach the block printing process. The students will print program covers.
- Assess students based on the Block Printing Evaluation rubric.
- With students, brainstorm ideas for costumes and scenery within cooperative groups.
- Conference with groups about individual responsibilities for costumes and scenery.
- Assess the costumes and scenery based on stated guidelines.
- Set up scenery for the rehearsals and performance with student help.
- Participate as part of the teaching team during the rehearsals and final performance.

Music Teacher Will:

- Introduce the concept of program music and review music vocabulary.
- Introduce the *Carnival of the Animals* music and apply research reports to identify which music represents each animal.
- Teach students to implement conducting patterns and musical analysis for each piece.
- Assess students based on the Music Assessment.
- Participate as part of the teaching team during the rehearsals and final performance.

Physical Education Teacher Will:

- Review change in levels and direction, locomotor and nonlocomotor movements, and variety of floor pattern (pathways).
- Introduce change in numbers (unison, opposition, and succession) and change in focus.
- Assign students to explore combinations of movements with the music.
- Conference with groups as they solve movement problems related to costumes and props.
- Assess students based on observations as well as how students apply the results of these observations to complete and refine their dance.
- Assess the dance using the Dance Assessment rubric.
- Participate as part of the teaching team during the rehearsals and final performance.

Resources:

Print
Amazing Animals of the World series. Danbury, Connecticut: Grolier, 1995.
Nature's Children series. Danbury, Connecticut: Grolier, 1999.
Ranger Rick. Reston, Virginia: National Wildlife Federation.
World Book Encyclopedia. Chicago: World Book, Inc., 2000.
Zoobooks Magazine. Poway, California: Wildlife Education, Ltd.

Electronic
Grolier Multimedia Encyclopedia. CD-ROM. Danbury, Connecticut: Grolier Interactive, 2000.

Audiovisuals
Saint-Saëns, Camille, comp. *Carnival of the Animals*. Charles Dutoit, cond. CD. Uni/London Classics, 1987.

Product or Culminating Activity: A public performance—using student-created dances, costumes, scenery, and programs—reveals enthusiastic student ownership of the work.

Assessment Overview: Animal Research—student self assesses using check sheets; library media specialist conferences with groups using check sheet. Block Printing Project—art teacher evaluates with rubric. Music Analysis Skills—music teacher assesses with a test. Dance Composition—physical education teacher assesses with a rubric and an observation check sheet. The final assessment is the performance itself.

Figure 4.16 **Carnival of Animals**

Animal Research Project Overview

The Basics

- This lesson begins our Carnival of Animals unit!
- You have listened to a recording of *Carnival of the Animals* by Camille Saint-Saëns.
- Each of you has been assigned to an animal group.
- Each of you has also been assigned an animal to portray in our upcoming student performance of Carnival of Animals, and your first assignment will be to research that animal during your library media center class each week.
- First we will review the research process; then you will read for information (to answer the research questions) and record the facts in your own words.
- It will probably take three to four class sessions for you to complete your "Animal Research Project."
- You will use your research results in art classes to help create costumes, program covers, and scenery.
- You will use your research results during physical education classes to develop dances depicting your animal.

Your Assignment

- You will conduct research about your assigned animal using nonfiction books, magazines, and electronic and science encyclopedias.
- You will locate and record facts about the appearance, movement, diet, and habitat of your animal.
- You will work cooperatively with other students in your assigned animal group.

Materials You Will Need

- A variety of learning resources including nonfiction books, magazines, and electronic and science encyclopedias.
- An "Animal Research Project" handout, listing questions to be answered about the appearance, movement, diet, and habitat of an animal.
- A student self-evaluation checklist.

How You Will Be Assessed

- You will complete a "Works Cited" sheet to indicate the resources used to locate information. You will record facts on the "Animal Research Project" handout, answering all questions. The library media specialist will read and evaluate all completed handouts.
- You will complete a self-evaluation checklist, which lists all the requirements of the lesson.
- The library media specialist will also observe you during class, watching for cooperative behaviors.

Figure 4.17 **Carnival of Animals**

Animal Research Project Checklist 1

Name _____ Class Code _____

Name of your animal _____ Date _____

Please fill in the following checklist to indicate your progress on the animal research project.

1. I have read about my animal and started to take notes. ❏ YES ❏ NO

 ■ I have information about my animal's description. ❏ YES ❏ NO

 ■ I have information about my animal's habitat. ❏ YES ❏ NO

 ■ I have information about my animal's behavior. ❏ YES ❏ NO

 ■ I have a picture of my animal. ❏ YES ❏ NO

2. I have used an electronic encyclopedia to conduct research. ❏ YES ❏ NO

 ■ When I used an electronic encyclopedia, I found useful ❏ YES ❏ NO
 information about my animal.

3. The next time we work on our research projects, I need to…

 ■ Read and take notes. ❏ YES ❏ NO

 ■ Locate and use additional resources. ❏ YES ❏ NO

 ■ Complete "Works Cited." ❏ YES ❏ NO

 ■ Write a rough draft. ❏ YES ❏ NO

How many resources have you used? 1 2 3 4 5

Figure 4.18   **Carnival of Animals**

Animal Research Project
Final Checklist

Name _____   Class Code _____

Name of your animal _____

❏   I have practiced highlighting important facts within an article about my animal.

❏   I have listed facts for each question on the research sheet.

❏   I have used at least three resources, including one electronic resource.

❏   I have listed the resources I used on the "Works Cited" sheet.

❏   I have a picture of my animal.

❏   I have worked with other members of my "animal group" during research sessions.

Figure 4.19   **Carnival of Animals**

Block Printing Project Overview

The Basics

■ This project will give you your first opportunity to apply the information you gained through your library research to your own artwork.

■ Our block printing project will require five 50-minute class sessions.

■ Your introduction to the project will be to look at a variety of prints. Our discussion of them will focus on details, composition, and expressions.

■ You will learn the process of block printing.

■ The art teacher will demonstrate:

- Transferring of sketch to block
- Tool safety and identification
- Block cutting process
- Inking and printing the block
- Editioning prints

■ You will focus on animal form, body proportion, expression, movement, other visual characteristics, and environmental surroundings.

■ You will work independently towards the completion of five editioned prints.

Your Assignment

■ Using illustrated reference books,, you will create four 4" × 6" preliminary sketches. Your peers and the Art Teacher will collaborate to help you refine and select one sketch to use for the printing project.

■ You will create a 4" × 6" composition based upon our Carnival of Animals theme and your research information. You will apply problem solving and creative thinking skills to do this.

■ You will create informative and appealing audience program covers.

■ You will incorporate your findings into scenery, creative dance movements, and coordinated costume design.

Materials You Will Need

■ Examples of block prints
■ 9 × 12 white drawing paper
■ Block Cutting Tools

■ Library Reference books
■ SAF-T-KUT Foam Blocks
■ Printing tools, ink—various colors

How You Will Be Assessed

■ You will submit one composition that applies research skills and reflects your understanding of illustrating your animal.

■ Your art teacher will observe your performance of the block cutting and printing process.

■ Your art teacher will evaluate your finished product based on pre-established guidelines.

Figure 4.20 **Carnival of Animals**

Block Printing Evaluation

Name _____ Homeroom _____

Animal group _____ Date _____

1=Needs Improvement   2=Satisfactory   3=Good   4=Excellent

	1	2	3	4
Composition				
Well-designed				
Illustrates application of research				
Block Cutting Process				
Demonstrated understanding of sketch transfer				
Demonstrated understanding of block cutting process				
Demonstrated safe use of tools				
Block Printing Process				
Demonstrated understanding of printing process				
Craftsmanship				
Demonstrated understanding of editioning prints				
Printed required number of editioned prints	Yes	No	Total Prints	

Teacher Comments:

Score:

Figure 4.21 **Carnival of Animals**

Music Lesson: An Analysis of Timbre, Phrasing, and Dynamics

The Basics

- This ongoing music lesson will require four 50-minute class sessions.
- The music teacher will introduce the concept of program music as it relates to *Carnival of the Animals* by Camille Saint-Saëns, i.e. that this is one long piece composed of many short pieces, each of which "describes" an animal through music.
- The music teacher will review meter and conducting patterns.
- You will listen to each short musical piece; however, we will focus our attention on the specific animals you have been assigned.
- The music teacher will identify the time signature of each piece and demonstrate the conducting of a few measures. You will count the number of measures in each piece, then determine the number and similarity of phrases.

Your Assignment

- You will learn the following concepts of music analysis through directed listening:
  - Timbre: You will identify the instruments used to portray that animal.
  - Phrasing: You will extend your knowledge of meter by determining the number and similarity of phrases in each piece.
  - Tempo and Dynamics: You will predetermine which tempo and dynamics would be appropriate for each piece.
- Through your research, you will be able to determine the appropriateness of the music to your animal.
- Through careful listening, you will be able to provide thoughtful analysis and bring creative ideas to the next phase of the project.

Materials You Will Need

- Check sheets and pencil for each student
- *Carnival of the Animals* CD
- CD Player
- Questionnaires
- Piano Score of *Carnival of the Animals*

How You Will Be Assessed

- You will fill out the checklist that asks specific questions about each piece.
- You will participate in creative discussion involving interpretation of your animal.
- You will generate ideas for use in physical education classes.

Figure 4.22 **Carnival of Animals**

Music Assessment

Name: _____ Class: _____

Using the vocabulary we have studied, answer the questions about the following *Carnival* pieces:

Timbre

1. Which instrument was used in the "FOSSILS"?   _____

2. Use an adjective to describe that instrument.   _____

3. Why is that timbre appropriate for describing fossils? _____

   _____

4. In which orchestral family is the instrument that is used to describe the elephant? _____

5. Does that instrument usually play the melody of a piece?   _____

6. Why is a flute a good choice for the birds? _____

   _____

Dynamics

7. In which piece are crescendo and decrescendo used most effectively?   _____

8. Where in this piece are these elements used?   _____

9. Would you use "piano" or "forte" to describe the swan?   _____

Tempo

10. Are the turtles "lento" or "allegro"?   _____

11. Are the donkeys "presto" or "largo"?   _____

Meter

12. Which three pieces seem to have no sense of meter? _____ _____ _____

13. Do you conduct the cuckoo in three or four?   _____

Miscellaneous

14. Which instrument plays the rooster? The cuckoo?   _____

15. The form of the "fossil" would best be described as AABA, ABA, rondo,
    or theme and variation **(circle one)**.

16. Which piece makes use of augmentation?   _____

17. Which piece best divides into obvious phrases?   _____

18. Would you describe the roosters and hens as "legato" or "staccato"?   _____

Figure 4.23   **Carnival of Animals**

Identifying Elements of Dance

The Basics

- The dance unit will be presented in combination with the gymnastics unit twice a week for five weeks.
- Your group will be rotated through dance (allowing use of two tape players) and gymnastics stations for four weeks.
- During the final week, all of our focus will be on the dance presentation.
- Additions or changes in movements must be adaptable to the costumes or props that you are making in art classes.
- Your group will address the issue of music interpretation.

Your Assignment

- You will improve your observation skills and accept constructive criticism for the purpose of improving your dance composition by:
  - Identifying locomotor movements.
  - Identifying nonlocomotor movements.
  - Making critical observations on a checksheet.
  - Using the checksheet to improve your dance through problem solving, reasoning, and creative thinking.
- Following this lesson, you will refine, polish, and practice your dance for the performance.
- Each group will critique one other group. You will look for variety of movement, a beginning and ending, and the movements' interpretation of the music.
- After exchanging and reviewing the checksheets, your group will make adjustments to your dance.

Materials You Will Need

- Checksheet and pencil
- Individual audio tapes of the music for your group
- Two tape players

How You Will Be Assessed

- The physical education teacher will use the checksheets to assess your knowledge and recognition of locomotor and nonlocomotor movements.
- A unit rubric will be used to measure your performance as a group member.

Figure 4.24 **Carnival of Animals**

Dance Evaluation

Name(s) _____ Class Code _____

Name of your animal _____ Date _____

Dance Assessment	Observed	Not Observed
Locomotor Skills		
Walk		
Hop		
Skip		
Gallop		
Jog		
Jump		
Slide		
Leap		
Nonlocomotor Movements		
Swing		
Twist		
Bend		
Stretch		
Pull		
Sway		
Turn		
Push		
Shake		
Rise		
Does the sequence have the following?		
Beginning		
3 Locomotor Movements		
3 Nonlocomotor Movements		
Ending		
Do the movements interpret the music?	**YES**	**NO**

Figure 4.25 **Carnival of Animals**

Dance Evaluation

Name(s) _____ Class Code _____

Name of your animal _____ Date _____

Rubric

Dance

■ To receive the grade "A" (excellent), the student must:

1. Offer suggestions.
2. Accept and try ideas from others.
3. Compromise to choose movements that interpret the words and music. Consider everyone's abilities and comfort.
4. Complete the movement composition within the time given.
5. Perform movements in rhythm to the music.
6. Complete an observation checklist of another group with at least 90% accuracy.
7. Demonstrate appropriate audience behavior.

■ To receive the grade "B" (good), the student must perform at least 6 of the above objectives.

■ To receive the grade "C" (satisfactory), the student must perform at least 5 of the above objectives.

■ To receive the grade "D" (poor, but passing), the student must perform at least 4 of the above objectives.

Castles: What Was Life Like?

Karen White, Librarian
Cheryl Morse, Grade 2 Teacher
Durham Elementary School
654 Hallowell Road, Durham, ME 04222
207-353-9333
kwhite42@gwi.net

Grade Levels: 2 and 7

Unit Overview: Castles: What Was Life Like? is a second grade research project that employs seventh graders to assist in library research, guided Web searching, and creation of a book about life in the Middle Ages. Each mixed-grade pair researches and writes about a different topic, chosen by the second grade partner. Seventh graders assist second graders to make a web with information located in the library and on the Internet, interpret difficult material, rewrite information in their own words, word process and print a final copy of their sentences, and illustrate their pages.

Time Frame: 5 weeks on a fixed schedule. Students meet for one 40-minute period per week in the library to research and create books and to conduct a guided Web search in the computer lab.

Content Area Standards: State of Maine Learning Results
<http://www.state.me.us/education/lres/lres.htm>

Social Studies, Elementary Level, Pre-K–2
Standard B. History: Students will develop historical knowledge of major events, people, and enduring themes in the United States, in Maine, and throughout world history.
B.1 Demonstrate an understanding of the similarities between families now and in the past, including daily life today and in other times.

English Language Arts, Middle Grades 5–8
Standard H. Research-Related Writing and Speaking: Students will work, write, and speak effectively when doing research in all content areas.
H.1 Collect and synthesize data for research topics from interviews and field work, using note taking and other appropriate strategies.
H.6 Use magazines, newspapers, dictionaries, journals, and other print sources to gather information for research topics.

Science and Technology, Middle Grades 5–8
Standard L: Communication: Students will communicate effectively in the application of science and technology.
L.6 Identify and perform roles necessary to accomplish group tasks.

Information Power Information Literacy Standards and Indicators: 1.1, 1.3, 1.4, 3.1, 3.2, 3.4, 9.1

Cooperative Teaching Plan:

Librarian Will:

- Create timeline and coordinate class activities during seventh grade weekly library class.
- Set up the computer lab appointment with the computer teacher.
- Clarify student expectations for seventh graders, i.e. location of information in library, creating a web, synthesizing information for younger audiences, creating computer pages.
- With Second Grade Teacher, establish groups, pairing for discipline, handicaps, etc.
- Provide an introduction to resources and teach research methods to seventh graders.
- Introduce seventh graders to collaborative methods for working with younger children.
- Assist in the actual research in the library.

Second Grade Teacher Will:

- Use the Know, Want to know, and Learned (KWL) activity to choose research topics.
- Assist students in the library and computer lab.
- Locate Web sites to be used in computer lab.
- Supervise completion of illustrations.
- Oversee the printing and collating of the book, one copy for each student.
- Work with the librarian and computer specialist to coordinate ideas, times, research, etc.

Resources:

Print

Aliki. *A Medieval Feast*. New York: Harper Collins, 1983.

Gibbons, Gail. *Knights in Shining Armor*. New York: Little Brown and Company, 1995.

Jordan, William Chester, ed. *The Middle Ages: An Encyclopedia for Students*. New York: Charles Scribner's Sons, 1996.

Langley, Andrew. *Medieval Life*. New York: Alfred A. Knopf, 1996.

Electronic

Castles of Britain. 1 July 2001. 5 July 2001 <http://www.castles-of-britain.com/>.

"Life in a Castle." *NOVA*. November 2000. 1 February 2002
>http://www.pbs.org/wgbh/nova/lostempires/trebuchet/castle.html>

Thomas, Jeffrey L. *Castles of Wales*. 1 July 2001. 5 July 2001
<http://www.castlewales.com/home.html>

Audiovisuals

The Middle Ages (NGS PicturePack Series Overheads). Washington, DC: National Geographic Society, 1995.

Product or Culminating Activity: The research is compiled as a chapter book about the Middle Ages that is unveiled at an Author's Tea where all students have a chance to share the book, autograph each other's books, have punch and cookies, and celebrate the end of the project.

Assessment Overview: Second graders complete a Library Self-Assessment rubric. Teacher assesses final chapters using traditional read-and-comment methods. Seventh graders complete Library and Computer Self-Assessment rubric. Computer/Technology Teacher assesses completed computer printout using student rubric responses and observation of independent work in the computer lab. Librarian assesses student using the Library Self-Assessment rubric.

Figure 4.26 **Castles: What Was Life Like?**

Library Self-Assessment Rubric—Grade 2

Name _____ Date _____

Topic Researched _____

Research Partner _____

Fill in the face that shows how you feel.

I feel the student and I worked well together.

We made a web from the information we found.

We wrote sentences about what we found.

I helped my partner illustrate the pages of our book.

The teacher's observations of what was happening.

Your Grade:

What did you like about this project?

_____

_____

What could be done to make this project better?

_____

_____

Figure 4.27   **Castles: What Was Life Like?**

Library Self-Assessment Rubric—Grade 7

Name _____ Date _____

Topic Researched _____

Research Partner/Job Done _____

Circle the number that you feel best reflects your experience:	**1=0**			**5=100**	
I feel that the student and I worked well together.	1	2	3	4	5
I helped the student locate information for his/her report.	1	2	3	4	5
I helped the student locate information on the Internet.	1	2	3	4	5
We made a web from the information we found.	1	2	3	4	5
We wrote sentences about what we found.	1	2	3	4	5
I typed the information on the computer.	1	2	3	4	5
I included the title, authors, who, what, where, when, why, and other interesting facts.	1	2	3	4	5
I passed in a copy of my final paper to my librarian and the teacher.	1	2	3	4	5
I helped the student illustrate his/her paper.	1	2	3	4	5
The teacher's observations of what was happening.	1	2	3	4	5
Your Grade:	1	2	3	4	5

What did you like about this project?

_____

_____

What could be done to make this project better?

_____

_____

Figure 4.28   **Castles: What Was Life Like?**

Computer Self-Assessment Rubric—Grade 7

Name _____   Date _____

Circle the number that reflects your experience.   **1=Not Very Well**   **5=Great Job**

I worked with a second grader searching for information on the Web.	1	2	3	4	5

I have created one page on the computer that includes the following:

Font is 14 to 18 points.	1	2	3	4	5
There are NO spelling errors (this is final copy).	1	2	3	4	5
Sentences begin with a capital and include ending punctuation.	1	2	3	4	5
Sentences are separated so they can be made into a book.	1	2	3	4	5
Both authors' names and the title are listed on title page.	1	2	3	4	5
Who	1	2	3	4	5
What	1	2	3	4	5
When	1	2	3	4	5
Where	1	2	3	4	5
Why	1	2	3	4	5
Interesting facts	1	2	3	4	5
I printed three copies for the librarian, the teacher, and the book.	1	2	3	4	5
I saved the information in case we need additional copies.	1	2	3	4	5
I turned in a copy of this evaluation to the librarian and the teacher. It is stapled to the copy of the sentences.	1	2	3	4	5

Figure 4.29   **Castles: What Was Life Like?**

Middle Ages Web

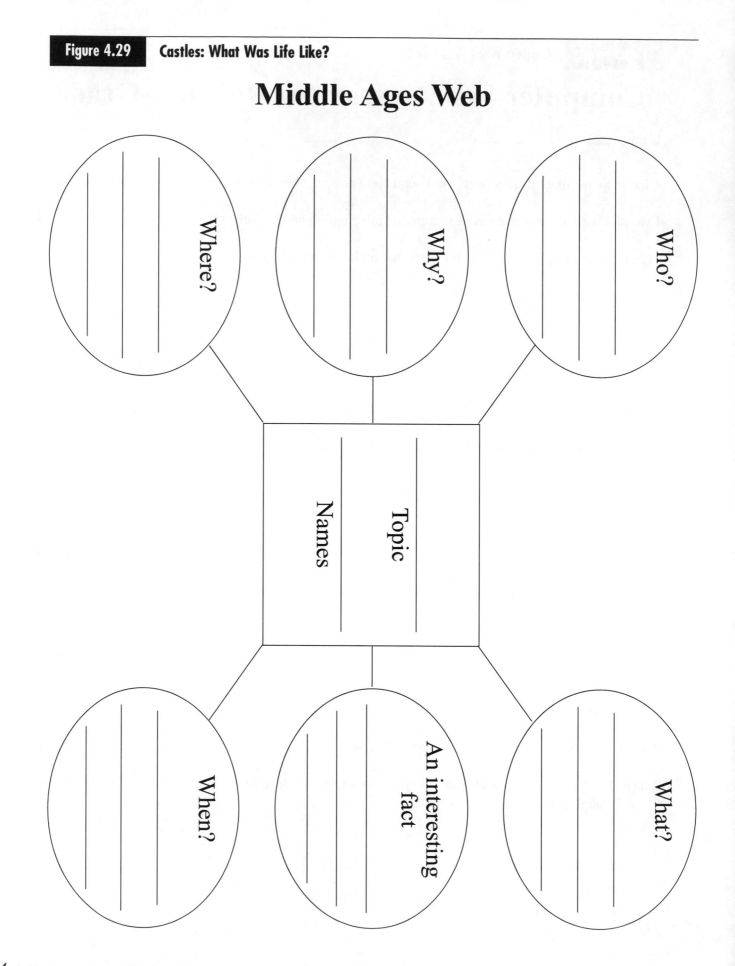

COMSI : Cedaroak Museum of Science and Industry

JoAnn Klassen, Library Media Specialist
Holly Grabow and Cheri Weaver, Fourth/Fifth Grade Teachers
Cedaroak Park School
4515 Cedaroak Drive, West Linn, OR 97068
503-673-7100
coplib@wlwv.k12.or.us
<http://www.wlwv.k12.or.us/cedaroak>

Grade Level: 4/5

Unit Overview: In COMSI <http://www.wlwv.k12.or.us/cedaroak/comsi>, students investigate a technological or scientific principle (e.g., optical illusion, Bernoulli's principle, gravity, animal tracking) through research. They write letters of inquiry and interview experts on their subject and related areas. They design experiments/demonstrations to investigate the topic. Students share their observational data and research findings with an audience through a demonstration and display. The idea created by Cheri Weaver has been enhanced and developed through collaboration with Holly Grabow, Teacher, and JoAnn Klassen, Library Media Specialist.

Time Frame: 6 to 8 weeks

Content Area Standards: State of Oregon Common Curriculum Goals and Academic Content Standards <http://www.open.k12.or.us/os2000/index.html>

Science
Scientific Inquiry: Use interrelated processes to pose questions and investigate the physical and living world.
Common Curriculum Goals: Formulate and express scientific questions and hypotheses to be investigated.
Content Standard: Formulate and express scientific questions and hypotheses to be investigated.
Grade 5 Benchmarks: Ask questions and make predictions that are based on observations and can be explored through simple investigations.
Content Standard: Use concepts and of: Evidence, models, and explanation.
Grade 5 Benchmarks: Use models to explain how objects, events, and/or processes work in the real world.
Content Standard: Formulate and express scientific questions and hypotheses to be investigated.
Grade 5 Benchmarks: Ask questions and make predictions that are based on observations and can be explored through simple investigations.

Science Unifying Concepts and Processes: Understand and apply major concepts and processes common to all sciences.

Common Curriculum Goal: Apply foundation concepts of change, cycle, cause and effect, energy and matter, evolution, perception, and fundamental entities.
Content Standard: Use concepts and of: Change, constancy, and measurement.
Grade 5 Benchmarks: Describe and explain different rates of change. Students will
   · identify and describe examples of rapid change and changes that happen at a slower pace.
   · identify and describe the changes people make in their environment.
   · identify and describe the human made and natural changes that occur in the environment; e.g. construction, fires and floods.
Common Curriculum Goal:. Use integrated scientific process skills to predict, design experiments, control variables, interpret data, define operations and formulate models.

English

Communication: Speak effectively for a variety of audiences and purposes and listen effectively to gather information.
Common Curriculum Goal: Communicate supported ideas using oral, visual, written, and multi-media forms in ways appropriate to topic, context, audience, and purpose.
Content Standard: Communicate knowledge of the topic, including relevant examples, facts, anecdotes, and details.
Grade 5 Benchmarks: Convey clear, focused main ideas with supporting details appropriate to audience and purpose.

Common Curriculum Goal: Structure oral, visual, written, and multi-media presentations in clear sequence, making connections and transitions among ideas and elements.
Content Standard: Structure information in clear sequence, making connections and transitions among ideas, sentences, and paragraphs.
Grade 5 Benchmarks: Demonstrate organization by developing a beginning, middle, and end with clear sequencing of ideas and transitions.

Common Curriculum Goal: Use the language, techniques, and conventions of a chosen communication form in ways appropriate to topic, context, audience, and purpose.
Content Standard: Select words that are correct, functional, and appropriate audience and purpose.
Grade 5 Benchmarks: Use descriptive and accurate appropriate to audience and purpose.

Information Power Information Literacy Standards and Indicators: 1.1, 1.2, 1.3, 1.4, 1.5, 2.1, 2.2, 2.3, 2.4, 3.1, 3.2, 3.3, 3.4

Cooperative Teaching Plan:

Library Media Specialist Will:
■ Assist students in making wise selections.
■ Provide a school library facility that is inviting and has an atmosphere that will encourage completion of this project.
■ Teach the information access skills that students need to be able to find the information.
■ Teach students multiple ways to record information and methods to cite resources.
■ Provide a collection of resources that will enable students to find information needed.
■ Provide time in a busy library schedule for each class and individual student to do research work necessary.

- Arrange class trips to do research at the public library and the middle school library.
- Support students in their efforts to create multimedia products for their projects, including but not limited to computer presentations (such as *HyperStudio* and *PowerPoint*) and video or audio recordings.
- Maintain a network of computers that allow students adequate access to Cedaroak Library catalog, online resources, and remote access to other libraries and to the Internet.
- Be available to assist students individually during the school day and before or after school by arrangement with students and their parents.
- Create and maintain a Web site for students to access online resources and access worksheets easily whether at home or at school.

Teachers Will:

- Design and implement an integrated assignment for the elementary school experience that leads to the state outcomes and challenges all children to think, research, speak, and perform at the highest possible level.
- Assist students in making wise selections and developing written proposals for declaring their topic/question on a scientific principle.
- Provide school time to research in the classroom, the school library, the middle school library, and the public library.
- Provide term calendars and assist students in breaking down the tasks and setting reasonable deadlines for these subtasks.
- Assist students in brainstorming possibilities for the creative design of experiments and demonstrations, learning centers, and in gathering school materials needed.
- Guide students in writing a complete bibliography.
- Provide format and time for practice runs in performing a live demonstration.
- Provide computer time to type written work, if needed.
- See to the preparation and setting up of the museum for THE NIGHT.
- Encourage students through a long and difficult (but exciting and empowering) process.

Resources:

Print

Ardley, Neil. *Dictionary of Science*. New York: Dorling Kindersley, 1994.

Barber, Jacqueline. *Chemical Reactions: Teacher's Guide*. Berkeley: University of California, Great Explorations in Math and Science (GEMS), 1986.

Blake, Jim. *The Great Perpetual Learning Machine: Being a Stupendous Collection of Ideas, Games, Experiments, Activities, and Recommendations for Further Exploration, with Tons of Illustrations*. Boston: Little, Brown, 1976.

The Dorling Kindersley's Science Encyclopedia. New York: Dorling Kindersley, 1993.

Downs, Robert B. *Landmarks in Science: Hippocrates to Carson*. Englewood, Colorado: Libraries Unlimited, 1982.

Gardner, Robert. *Experiments with Motion*. Springfield, N.J. : Enslow Publishers, 1995.

Goldstein-Jackson, Kevin. *Experiments with Everyday Objects: Science Activities for Children, Parents, and Teachers*. Englewood Cliffs, N.J.: Prentice-Hall, 1978.

Junior Science Experiments on File. New York: Facts on File, 1993.

Moran, Mike. *KidSource: Science Fair Handbook*. Los Angeles: Lowell House Juvenile, 1998.

The Raintree Illustrated Science Encyclopedia. Milwaukee: Raintree Publishers, 1984.

Stone, Jeanne. *Simon and Schuster Illustrated Dictionary of Science*. New York: Wanderer Books, 1985.

Travers, Bridget, ed. *World of Scientific Discovery*. Detroit: Gale, 1994.

Twist, Clint. *Rain to Dams Projects with Water*. New York: Gloucester Press, 1990.

VanCleave, Janice Pratt. *Janice VanCleave's Machines: Mind-boggling Experiments You Can Turn into Science Fair Projects*. New York: Wiley, 1993.

VanCleave, Janice Pratt. *Chemistry for Every Kid: 101 Easy Experiments That Really Work*. New York: Wiley, 1989.

Webster, Vera R. *Plant Experiments*. Chicago: Childrens Press, 1982.

The World of Science. New York: Facts On File, 1984–1986.

Electronic

"Ask a Scientist." *ALCOM Education Project*. 31 July 2001
    <http://olbers.kent.edu/alcomed/Ask/ask.html>.

"Homework Center." *Multnomah County Library*. 31 July 2001
    <http://www.multnomah.lib.or.us/lib/homework/index.html>.

"KidsClick! Web Search for Kids by Librarians." *Sun Site*. 31 July 2001
    <http://sunsite.berkeley.edu/KidsClick!/>.

Primary and Middle Search Online. EBSCO Publishing. Requires subscription.

"Science Fair Central: Creative Investigations into the Real World." *Discovery School.Com*. 31 July 2001 <http://school.discovery.com/sciencefaircentral/>.

World Book Online. 31 July 2001 <http://www.worldbookonline.com/>. Requires subscription.

Audiovisual

A variety of VHS films borrowed from a centralized video library upon student request.

Supplies

Students are limited to materials that they can find and borrow. Each must submit a budget not to exceed $15 for purchased materials.

Product or Culminating Activity: Simulating the Oregon Museum of Science and Industry <http://www.omsi.org> format of displays and demonstrations, students will share their expertise with parents and guests in a schoolwide COMSI event. In preparation, students rehearse demonstrations extensively in pairs and then in front of the whole class. Classmates simulate questions that adults might ask, putting themselves in the "hotseat." Students wear lab coats and choose a creative alias that represents the concept studied, i.e., Dr. Seismo Graph (Earthquake) or Professor Bubble.

Assessment Overview: With an emphasis on process rather than product, teachers evaluate students throughout the process using the Weekly Update. Completion of the display and demonstration reveals student understanding of the individual concept studied. The Assessment Sheet serves as an inventory of required display components, and the Display Rubric helps students improve the quality of the display. In addition, students complete the Self Evaluation sheet. The library media specialist evaluates the List of Citations using the Checklist. Finally, each student creates a question and completes the compiled quiz questions representing each student's work.

Figure 4.30   COMSI: Cedaroak Museum of Science and Industry

Task Analysis

CHOOSING TOPIC TO INVESTIGATE

- Visit COMSI and complete scavenger hunt
- Participate in "read around."
- Do quick search for ideas.
- Browse topics in Web site
  <http://school.discovery.com/sciencefaircentral/scifairstudio/ideas.html>.

GATHERING INFORMATION

- Use library catalog to find out what we have.
- Use online resources (World Book Encyclopedia Online, EBSCO Primary or Middle Search).
- Search the Internet through KidsClick < http://sunsite.berkeley.edu/KidsClick!/>.
- Search the online film catalog.
- Take notes from texts.

LETTER(S) OF INQUIRY: (1 REQUIRED)

- Brainstorm (think of many possibilities).
- Find addresses.
- Draft letter.
- Word process final copy of letter (print 2 copies of each letter).
- Address an envelope.
- Send the letter and wait for reply!

INTERVIEW(S): (1 REQUIRED)

- Brainstorm many possibilities.
- Contact possible interviewees (you may use adult help).
- Develop questions.
- Practice interview with a buddy.
- Do interview.
- Find a way to use/share the information.

MUSEUM DEMONSTRATION

- Brainstorm possible experiments/demonstrations (for you to do or for your audience to participate in).
- Gather materials.
- Practice alone and then for a buddy.
- Demonstrate for the class ("hotseat").

Figure 4.30   **(continued from page 76)**

WORK CITED

- Keep track of sources.
- Put in correct form (Library Media Specialist will OK).
- Make a final copy on the computer.
- Mount and display.

COSTUMES

- Locate lab coat to wear (hint: your teacher has borrowed many).
- Make COMSI badge.

DISPLAY

- Brainstorm possible things to include (together).
- Select types of items to include.
- Think of a background structure for display (be creative).
- Sketch and label possible display (you may wish to change and adapt along the way).
- Gather materials.
- Create labels and captions.
- Mount items on display.

ASSESSMENT

- Evaluate the display using display rubric.
- Read your teacher's assessment and comments.

Figure 4.31   **COMSI: Cedaroak Museum of Science and Industry**

Sample Subjects and Burning Questions

- What are the **six simple machines** and how do they work?
- How do **pulleys, levers, and gears** affect the way machines work?
- What are **tides**? What causes them and what is their impact?
- How do **batteries** work?
- How did **dinosaurs evolve** through prehistoric times?
- How do the **tools** work that **spies** use?
- How do **bridges** hold their weight?
- How are **stalactites and stalagmites** formed?
- What are **gases** and their uses?
- How are **tsunamis** formed?
- Why do different types of **volcanoes** erupt?
- How do **optical illusions** fool the eye?
- What is the **eye** and how does it function?
- How does the **brain** use information from the senses?
- What is the **heart** and how does it work?
- How does a **saltwater marine environment** differ from a **fresh water marine environment**?
- How does an **MRI** work?
- How are **fireworks** constructed?
- How do **dolphins** communicate?
- What is **sodium bicarbonate** and what does it do?
- How do **birds** fly?
- What causes **earthquakes**?
- Why does white light go through a prism and come out the colors that it does? **(color/light)**
- What are **hurricanes**?
- How do **crystals** form?
- What causes **lightning** to form?
- What are the differences between **acids and bases**?
- How can we help **save water** and prevent drought?
- How do **mammals survive the winter**?
- How do **nocturnal animals (particularly bats) maneuver** at night? **(echo location)**
- How does **electromagnetism** run motors?
- What is a **comet**? What kind of damage can it do to the Earth?
- How do complex **electrical circuits** work?
- How do manufactured things **hover**?
- What conditions best create **static electricity**?
- How do bones get **calcium** and use it?
- How do **black holes** form and how do they behave?
- Which rodent is the easiest to train in a maze? **(Animals used in research)**
- How does **photosynthesis** make leaves change color?

Figure 4.32   **COMSI: Cedaroak Museum of Science and Industry**

The Art of Interviewing

Each of you is responsible for interviewing at least one person.
To choose a person to interview you must consider a few questions:

- Can you interview this person in person or will it have to be over the phone?
- Do you want to interview a person who knows about the subject through their work or do you want to interview a person who can relate in some way to your burning question?
- Who do you know who might put you into contact with someone to interview (this is called networking)?
- When might you have time to set up the interview and what steps will it take to set up the interview?
- What questions will you ask and how will you record the answers?

Below is space to get yourself organized and on the road to a successful interview. Also ask your teacher or the library media specialist to help you brainstorm ideas.

List 3 people or places you might call for an interview:

_____

_____

_____

When are you not available for the interview? (Consider your parents' schedule if they will be driving you to the interview).

_____

_____

_____

Think of at least 5 questions you'd like to ask:

_____

_____

_____

_____

_____

_____

Figure 4.32   **(continued from page 82)**

How will these questions help you get to know your character better?

_____

_____

What would be appropriate to wear to an interview such as this?

_____

_____

I would highly recommend that you take a tape recorder so you can concentrate on what the person is saying and what would be a logical next question.

Do you need to borrow a tape recorder from the school library? Yes_____No_____

Do you have the address of the interviewee, so you can write a thank-you note and send an invitation? What is the address?

_____

_____

Tips for a good interview:

1. Introduce yourself, shake hands, and smile when first meeting the person. Be sure to thank him/her for this opportunity at the start. He/She may have questions about our project. If you take your contract along that might help. Also, be prepared to briefly explain what happens during COMSI.
2. Ask for permission to tape the interview. If he/she is not comfortable with this, graciously go along with his/her preference, but ask for patience as you take notes.
3. Try to look your interviewee in the eye as much as possible.
4. Be prepared with written questions.
5. You want your questions to flow in a logical sequence, for example, all questions about how something works and the tasks they do in their job. Start with a question you know he/she can answer.
6. Listen to what your interviewee has to say so you can avoid asking a question he/she has already answered (even if it is on your written list of questions).
7. You will probably want to finally ask whether he/she has ideas about others you might contact. This is called networking.
8. Thank the interviewee for his/her time. If you have an invitation to COMSI with you, this would be an appropriate time to give it.
9. Send a letter of thanks after you get back.
10. After you get home, you will need to listen to the tape so you can take notes. Some of you will want to "transcribe" the tape (write or type out the dialog).
11. You may wish to use the tape or the transcription in your display.

Figure 4.33 **COMSI: Cedaroak Museum of Science and Industry**

Weekly Update

Name _____ Topic_____

Date Due _____ Parent Signature _____

My *burning question* is _____

_____

RESOURCES: I have found the following **new** resources:(could include):

Computer resources: EBSCO _____World Book Online _____

Internet through KidsClick _____

A video: yes _____ no _____ Title _____

Books _____

_____

Other _____

LETTERS:

I have sent _____ new letters of inquiry this week.

I have sent a total of _____ letters of inquiry so far.

INTERVIEW:

I have planned an interview with _____

Day _____ Time _____

I have written my interview questions: yes _____ no _____ (please attach)

I need to borrow a tape recorder: yes _____ no _____

I have already conducted an interview with _____

Figure 4.33 **(continued from page 84)**

WORKS CITED:

PLEASE ATTACH WHAT YOU HAVE ACCUMULATED FOR WORKS CITED SO FAR. You may attach your Citation Worksheet Grid if you'd like. Also, you should have already started word processing this in proper form and continue to add as you go.

EXPERIMENTS/DEMONSTRATIONS:

These are experiments or demonstrations I plan to do for COMSI night:

1. _____

2. _____

3. _____

4. _____

AUDIENCE INTERACTIONS: I will involve my audience by:

1. _____

2. _____

3. _____

DISPLAY: Please attach your sketch for your display (please see display sheet for required elements.)

GENERAL INFORMATION:

Share anything here that you have worked on towards your COMSI project that you'd like me to know:

_____

_____

_____

_____

_____

_____

Figure 4.33   **(continued from page 85)**

TIME:

Approximate time you've spent this week on COMSI:

At home:

Fri. _____ Sat. _____ Sun. _____ Mon. _____ Tues. _____ Wed. _____ Thurs. _____

At school:

Fri. _____ Mon. _____ Tues. _____ Wed. _____ Thurs. _____

OR

Use your time graph to show the total for the week.

At home: _____   At school: _____

PLANNING:

What do you plan to accomplish next week? _____

_____

_____

_____

QUESTIONS YOU MIGHT HAVE FOR ME:

| Figure 4.34 | COMSI: Cedaroak Museum of Science and Industry |

Display Requirements

ITEMS	INCLUDED
Copy of letters sent	_____
Letters returned (if you have any)	_____
■ *Interview documentation	_____
■ *Works Cited (formally written in proper form)	_____
■ *Process work (Updates, contract, etc.)	_____
■ *Financial Statement	_____
■ *Credits	_____

**************REAL WORLD CONNECTION*************

Pictures/captions (written by YOU)	_____
■ *Title and burning question	_____
■ Factoids	_____
■ Flip questions	_____
■ Glossary specific to your topic	_____
■ Diagrams/graphs/charts	_____
■ Hyperstudio	_____
■ Electric box	_____
■ Games	_____
■ Directions for independent audience interactions	_____
■ Other creative ideas you have	_____

*Required items

| Figure 4.35 | COMSI: Cedaroak Museum of Science and Industry |

Display Rubric

SUPERB:

- Display is creative, unique, and attention getting.
- Display shows conceptual understanding and real world connection.
- Display is my own work.
- There is a clear title and creator's name.
- There are labels and captions as needed.
- Citations, credits and letters are visible.
- A small amount of photocopied work is evident, if any.
- Question and answer element and art element are included and well done.
- Penmanship is neat, reasonably sized, in ink or typed, and well-edited.
- Work is matted or framed, neat, glued down, and there are no erasure marks.
- Space is used attractively, not overcrowded, colorful and three-dimensional.
- I tried my best.

GREAT:

- There is a title, creator's name, labels, and captions.
- Display shows knowledge of subject.
- Citations, credits and letters are visible.
- Display is my own work (assistance given when absolutely necessary).
- A large amount of photocopied work is evident.
- All (except perhaps one) of the requirements are evident.
- There are some misspellings or mechanics mistakes.
- There is a little overcrowding of materials or empty space.
- Glue is showing, work is crooked, and erasure marks or whiteout shows.
- Good editing is evident.
- I tried my best.

ACCOMPLISHED:

- I met most of the requirements. One or more of the following is missing:
  - Citations
  - Letters sent
  - Interview documentation
  - Credits
  - Financial statement
  - Questions and answers (science folder, Hypercard, flip cards)
  - Title, creator's name, labels, and captions
  - Editing
  - Polish
- Display is mostly my work.
- I tried my best.

Figure 4.36   **COMSI: Cedaroak Museum of Science and Industry**

Assessment Sheet

Name _____ Topic_____

Requirements:

_____ title, scientist's name   _____ burning questions

_____ credits   _____ financial statement

_____ interview documentation   _____ letters of inquiry

_____ real world connection   _____ factoids

_____ process pieces

_____ written captions for all my pictures

_____ written instruction for audience interaction, if independent

Extras:

_____ electric box   _____ letter responses

_____ HyperStudio   _____ slide show

_____ posters   _____ souvenirs

_____ quotes   _____ vocabulary

_____ game   _____ comment sheets

_____ other:

Display Guidelines:

_____ Labels and captions as needed

_____ Only a small amount of photocopied work evident, if necessary

_____ Well-edited

_____ Work is neat, glued well, no erasure marks

_____ Matted, color scheme, tidy presentation of materials

_____ Space used attractively, not overcrowded, colorful and three-dimensional

_____ Display is my own work

_____ I did my best

Comments:

Figure 4.37   COMSI: Cedaroak Museum of Science and Industry

Citations Checklist

Citations Checklist (10 pts)

_____ Hanging indent (2 points)

_____ Alphabetical order

_____ Title centered

_____ Punctuation

_____ Capitalization

_____ Citations complete (2 points)

_____ Space after each citation

_____ Spelling

Figure 4.38 **COMSI: Cedaroak Museum of Science and Industry**

Self Evaluation

Name _____ Date _____

Professional Name _____

1. The concept I chose was (easy/hard to research…etc). Explain why.

2. How well did I manage my time? Did I stay ahead of schedule? Was I stressed or relaxed? Why? What did I learn about managing my time? How would I plan differently next time?

3. How well did I research? What research method worked best for me? Why? What note gathering method worked best for me? (notecards…sheets of paper…Middle school sheets with citation info on the top…color coding…highlighting…etc.). Why? What did I learn about researching? What would I do differently on the next research project?

4. What did I learn from my research that I thought was most interesting?

Food for the Community and You
Faith A. Delaney, Library Media Specialist
Lauren Buchman, Grade 6 Teacher
Mary Shawkey, Family & Consumer Science Teacher; Tom Bechtel, Tech Ed
Wheatland Middle School
919 Hamilton Park Drive, Lancaster, PA 17603
717- 291-6125
Fdelaney@lancaster.k12.pa.us

Grade Level: 6

Unit Overview: In Food for the Community and You, students will organize and implement a food drive to benefit an area in their community. Students will study food groups and healthy diets. Students will then research hunger in their community and select a group to receive the food donation. Students will advertise the food drive and collect donations. The collection site will include a physical model of the Food Guide Pyramid, designed and built by the students. Food will be collected and displayed in the Food Guide Pyramid prior to distribution.

Time Frame: Five weeks.

Content Area Standards: Proposed Academic Standards for Civics and Government, Pennsylvania Department of Education <http://www.pde.psu.edu/standard/civics.pdf>

5.2.6 Rights and Responsibilities of Citizenship, Grade 6
A. Compare rights and responsibilities of citizenship
Personal responsibility of the individual to society.
D. Describe the importance of political leadership and public service.

Proposed Academic Standards for Health, Safety and Physical Education, Pennsylvania Department of Education < http://www.pde.psu.edu/standard/hspewhole.pdf>

10.1.6 Concepts of Health, Grade 6
B. Analyze nutritional concepts that impact health.

Adopted Academic Standards for Science and Technology, Pennsylvania Department of Education, Pending Review <http://www.pde.psu.edu/standard/science.pdf>

3.7.4 Technological Devices, Grade 4
A. Explore the use of basic tools, simple materials and techniques to safely solve problems
B. Select appropriate instruments to study materials

Information Power Information Literacy Standards and Indicators: 4.1, 4.2, 9.1, 9.2, 9.3, 9.4

Cooperative Teaching Plan:

Library Media Specialist Will:
- Collect print and nonprint resources to implement the Food Bank Unit.
- Introduce the Food Bank Project (with sixth grade FCS and Tech Ed. teachers).
- Schedule classes in the media center.
- Assist students in developing appropriate search strategies.
- Assist students in searching for information in print and electronic sources.
- Guide and conference individually with students during the research process (with sixth grade and FCS teachers).
- Contact a local speaker to address classes.
- Contact local food bank selected for donations and arrange for pickup or delivery.
- Contact local newspaper or television station to publicize the students' achievement.

Classroom Teacher Will:
- Draw up a time frame for the unit (with LMS, FCS, and Tech. Ed. teachers).
- Introduce the Food Bank Project (with LMS, FCS teachers).
- Discuss what students know and would like to know about hunger in the community.
- Discuss the problem of hunger both nationally and locally.
- Assist students in locating several food donation sites in the community.
- Schedule a speaker for a class period.
- Encourage students to choose (vote on) the site they will use for their food donations.
- Assist students in planning and implementing an advertising campaign for the food drive (could work with the art teacher on this).

Family & Consumer Science (FCS) Teacher Will:
- Schedule classes for students to learn about food and nutrition (with sixth grade teacher).
- Instruct students about the Food Guide Pyramid and dietary guidelines for good health.
- Distribute students' workbook.
- Monitor entries in students' workbook.
- Discuss each day's food collection and help students choose where to place the items on the physical model of the pyramid (with sixth grade teacher).
- Display each day's donated food in appropriate spaces on the model of the food pyramid. Remove foods on the model and box for pickup at the end of the day.

Technology Education Teacher Will:
- Schedule classes for students to plan and build the Food Pyramid Model (with sixth grade teacher).
- Assist students in planning and designing a physical model of the food pyramid (must be transportable, must include shelves for each food group, and so on).
- Help students generate a list of materials needed to build the model.
- Purchase materials needed.
- Instruct students in safety and use of tools.
- Oversee the building of the model by students.

Resources:

Print

Evers, Connie. *How to Teach Nutrition to Kids: An Integrated Creative Approach to Nutrition Education For Children Ages 6–10*. Portland, Oregon: 24 Carrot Press, 1996.

Food Guide Pyramid. Washington, DC: USDA, 1996. (Available from Superintendent of Documents Consumer Information Center Dept. 159-Y Pueblo, Colorado 81009.)

Kalbacken, Joan. *The Food Pyramid*. New York: Children's Press, 1998.

Local telephone book (look under Human Service Agencies/Food Resources to find a guest speaker and to select the site the students want to receive donations).

Electronic

"Food Guide Pyramid." *American Dietetic Association*. 23 July 2001 <http://www.eatright.org/fgp.html>.

"The Food Guide Pyramid; A Guide to Daily Food Choices." *National Agricultural Library*. 23 July 2001 < http://www.nalusda.gov:8001/py/pmap.htm>.

"The Food Pyramid; A Plan for Eating." *Franklin Institute Online*. 23 July 2001 <http://www.fi.edu/biosci/healthy/pyramid.html>.

"Hunger & Poverty Facts." *World Hunger Year (WHY)*. 23 July 2001 <http://worldhungeryear.org/hun_pov/default.asp>.

Levine, Larry and Jane Finn Levine. *Kids Can Make a Difference*. 23 July 2001 <http://www.kids.maine.org/>.

Pyramid Challenge: A CD-ROM Healthy Eating Guide. CD-ROM. Amherst, New York: DINE Systems, Inc., 1996.

"USDA Food Pyramid." *Encarta 1999*. CD-ROM, Redmond, WA: Microsoft, 1999.

Worthington-Roberts, Bonnie. "Human Nutrition." *Encarta 1999*. CD-ROM. Redmond, WA: Microsoft, 1999.

Audiovisuals

Eat Smart. Videocassette. Educational Video Network, 1994.

Film footage on community needs reported by local TV station(s).

Guest Speaker

Representative from local food bank or similar community organization visits school to talk about hunger in the community.

Product or Culminating Activity: Students make a visual representation of the Food Guide Pyramid and advertise and collect food for a food drive. Students donate the food to their chosen group.

Assessment Overview: Final assessments for this unit are shared by all teachers involved. The tech ed. reacher will grade the physical model of the Food Guide Pyramid using the instructional rubric for both model building and safety guidelines. The family and consumer science teacher will assess the student's knowledge of nutrition based on the rubric concerned with personal nutrition and on the pages in the student workbook on nutrition. The library media specialist and the sixth grade teacher will collaborate on assessing the research portion of the unit, the teacher focusing on the content and the library media specialist focusing on the quality and quantity of the sources located.

Figure 4.39   **Food for the Community and You**

Instructional Rubric: Research and Food Drive

Name _____

	SELF	PEER	TEACHER
I have located and read information from three sources on hunger in our community.	Y NY	Y NY	Y NY
I have written an action plan that could impact the issue.	Y NY	Y NY	Y NY
I have completed a cause-and-effect chart for each action plan.	Y NY	Y NY	Y NY
I have listed local organizations that provide for people in need in our community.	Y NY	Y NY	Y NY
I have listed organizations and groups that need food in our community.	Y NY	Y NY	Y NY
I have helped to select a group to receive food.	Y NY	Y NY	Y NY
I have helped to choose the date(s) for the food drive.	Y NY	Y NY	Y NY
We have determined the extent of our food drive campaign.	Y NY	Y NY	Y NY
We have developed appropriate publicity for our target audience.	Y NY	Y NY	Y NY
We have advertised to our target group.	Y NY	Y NY	Y NY
We have collected and displayed the food in our pyramid model.	Y NY	Y NY	Y NY
We have donated the food to our chosen group.	Y NY	Y NY	Y NY

STUDENT: _____   PEER: _____

COMMENTS:

Figure 4.40   **Food for the Community and You**

Instructional Rubric: Personal Nutrition

	SELF	PEER	TEACHER
I have found two food labels illustrating the Food Guide Pyramid.	Y NY	Y NY	Y NY
I have read an article discussing the Food Guide Pyramid.	Y NY	Y NY	Y NY
I have made a visual representation of the Food Guide Pyramid.	Y NY	Y NY	Y NY
We have chosen one of the Dietary Guidelines for Good Health and presented this guideline to the class.	Y NY	Y NY	Y NY
I have defined the six food groups.	Y NY	Y NY	Y NY
I have planned a one day personal diet that reflects my understanding of the Food Guide Pyramid and the Dietary Guidelines for Good Health.	Y NY	Y NY	Y NY

STUDENT: _____ PEER: _____

COMMENTS:

Figure 4.41   **Food for the Community and You**

Instructional Rubric: Personal Nutrition

	SELF	PEER	TEACHER
We have selected a design of a scaled model of the Food Guide Pyramid.	Y NY	Y NY	Y NY
We have selected the appropriate materials with which to build the model.	Y NY	Y NY	Y NY
I have been observed following safety rules at my station.	Y NY	Y NY	Y NY
I have been observed exhibiting on-task behavior at my station.	Y NY	Y NY	Y NY
I have participated in the building of the model. We have completed and submitted our model for approval.	Y NY	Y NY	Y NY

STUDENT: _____ PEER: _____

COMMENTS:

Figure 4.42   **Food for the Community and You**

Assessment Rubric: Research

Performance Activity: You will research information on hunger in your community, organize and implement a food drive, and choose a group to receive the food donation.

Performance Activity Assessment Rubric

Exceptional	Identifies community problems and locates and reads information from more than three sources including a variety of media	Describes two or more courses of action that impact on a community issue using examples	Identifies more than one positive effect and more than one negative effect of a course of action with supporting rationale
Commendable	Identifies community problems and locates and reads information from three sources independently	Describes two or more courses of action that impact on a community issue	Identifies more than one positive effect and more than one negative effect of a course of action
Satisfactory	Identifies community problems and locates and reads information from three sources with guidance	Describes one course of action that impacts on a community issue	Identifies one positive and one negative effect of a course of action
Unsatisfactory	Does not identify community problems or locate and read information from three sources	Does not describe a course of action that impacts on a community issue	Does not identify a positive or negative effect of a course of action

Figure 4.43   **Food for the Community and You**

Assessment Rubric: Personal Nutrition

Performance Activity: Study food groups and healthy diets. Demonstrate an understanding of the Food Guide Pyramid and Dietary Guidelines for Good Health and plan a healthy personal diet.

Performance Activity Assessment Rubric

Exceptional	Names the six food groups, explains the concept of the food pyramid, and compares it to one other food guide	Identifies the Dietary Guidelines for Good Health, explains their relationship to good health, and elaborates on the consequences of ignoring them	Plans a personal diet for one day that reflects the pyramid and guidelines and describes the impact that following that diet would have on his or her health
Commendable	Names the six food groups and explains the concept of the food pyramid	Identifies the Dietary Guidelines for Good Health and explains their relationship to good health	Plans a personal diet for one day that reflects the pyramid and guidelines and names the lifestyle changes needed
Satisfactory	Names the six food groups and categorizes food into each group	Identifies the Dietary Guidelines for Good Health	Plan a personal diet for one day that reflects the pyramid and guidelines
Unsatisfactory	Does not name the six food groups or categorize food into each group	Does not identify the Dietary Guidelines for Good Health	Does not plan a personal diet for one day that reflects the pyramid and guidelines

Figure 4.44 **Food for the Community and You**

Assessment Rubric: Visual Representation of the Food Guide Pyramid

Performance Activity: Organize and implement a food drive to benefit your community. The collection site will include a physical model of the Food Guide Pyramid that you designed and built.

Performance Activity Assessment Rubric

Exceptional	Visually pleasing model of the Food Group Pyramid	Accompanying materials for publicity to increase scope of food drive	Food collected outside of the school to represent all food groups	Choose a community group to receive the food donation
Commendable	Labeled physical model of the Food Group Pyramid	Labeled with additional nutritional information	Food collected school-wide to represent all food groups	Choose a community group to receive the food donation
Satisfactory	Labeled physical model of the Food Group Pyramid	Labeled	Food collected from the class to represent all food groups	Choose a community group to receive the food donation

Figure 4.45 **Food for the Community and You**

Assessment Rubric: Safety Procedures

Performance Activity: Design and build a physical model of the Food Guide Pyramid for the collection site with attention to proper use of tools and materials and safety procedures.

Performance Activity Assessment Rubric

Exceptional	Consistently follows prescribed safety procedures and suggests improved safety measures	Consistently focuses attention on task/activity and monitors the area to minimize distractions
Commendable	Consistently follows prescribed safety procedures and reminds others to work safely	Consistently focuses attention on task/activity and avoids distracting others
Satisfactory	Consistently follows prescribed safety procedures	Consistently focuses attention on task/activity
Unsatisfactory	Does not follow prescribed safety procedures	Does not consistently focus attention on task/activity

History Fair
Abigail Garthwait, Library Media Specialist
Dian Jordan, Grade 5 Teacher
Asa Adams Elementary School
10 Goodridge Drive, Orono, ME 04473
207-866-2151
abigail@umit.maine.edu

Grade Level: 5

Unit Overview: After reading a historical fiction book of their choice, fifth grade students develop "burning questions" about the time period, which they seek to answer. The library media specialist teaches more complex ways to perform library and Internet research, building on what students have previously learned. History Fair is the culminating activity, which consists of student projects, displayed on tables arranged in chronological order in the gym. Students dress in period costumes, and classes of younger students tour the fair. An evening open house allows students to share their newly-found knowledge with adults—both parents and community members.

Time Frame: 8 weeks

Content Area Standards: State of Maine Learning Results
<http://www.state.me.us/education/lres/lres.htm>

Social Studies: History, Middle Grades 5–8
Standard B. Historical Knowledge, Concepts and Patterns: Students will develop historical knowledge of major events, people and enduring themes in the United States, in Maine and throughout world history.
B.1 Demonstrate an understanding of the causes and effects of major events in United States History and the connections to Maine history with an emphasis on events up to 1877, including but not limited to: Declaration of Independence; The Constitution; Westward Expansion; Industrialization; Civil War.

English Language Arts, Middle Grades 5–8
Standard A. Process of Reading: Students will use the skills and strategies of the reading process to comprehend, interpret, evaluate and appreciate what they have read.
A.1 Formulate questions to be answered while reading.
A.5 Understand stories and expository texts from the perspective of the social and cultural context in which they were created.
A.9 Explain orally and defend opinions formed while reading and viewing.

Standard F. Standard English Conventions: Students will write and speak correctly, using conventions of standard written and spoken English.
F.1 Edit written work for standard English spelling and usage.

F.2 Demonstrate command of the conventions necessary to make an informal speech or presentation, effectively engaging peers and fielding responses.

Information Power Information Literacy Standards and Indicators: 1.3, 1.5, 2.1, 2.4, 3.4, 9.1

Cooperative Teaching Plan:

Note: This school maintains an online library catalog, but at the time of this unit, there was not an adequate number of terminals available for student use, so the card catalog was kept fully up-to-date and students were taught to use it.

Library Media Specialist Will:

- Teach the concept of locating historical fiction by time period. (This extends students' knowledge of subject level searches, particularly in the tricky area of History. With the advent of keyword searching online, the lessons revolving around finding appropriate material have become less frustrating to students. Nevertheless it's still an important search strategy.)
- Approve student selection of a historical novel (with teacher).
- Present resources and strategies relevant to this assignment.
- Teach full group lessons on Internet searching and periodical index use.
- Review strategies for utilization of resources.
- Help students to revise burning questions of personal interest about the time period.
- Verify students' ability to use efficient search strategies.
- Assist in the classroom during the student creation of visual projects.
- Prepare for, supervise, and participate in the History Fair (with teacher).

Teacher Will:

- Introduce project in the classroom, with goals and expectations.
- Approve student selection of a historical novel (with LMS).
- Evaluate student "book report," which includes a summary and reflection.
- Supervise student compilation of four or five burning questions of personal interest about the time period.
- Orchestrate student writing of a research report and creation of a visual project related to what they have learned.
- Assess student research report with a rubric.
- Prepare for and supervise the History Fair (with LMS).

Resources:

Print

An abundant supply of quality historical fiction and nonfiction history books, including:
Fiction authors, such as Avi, the Collier brothers, Pam Conrad, Christopher Paul Curtis, Paula Fox, Kathryn Laskey, Lois Lowry, Scott O'Dell, Ann Rinaldi, Elizabeth George Speare, Rosemary Sutcliff, Mildred Taylor, Theodore Taylor, Anne Turner, Yoshiko Uchida, Yoko Watkins, Jane Yolen, and **Nonfiction authors,** such as Leonard Everett Fisher, Russell Freedman, Jean Fritz, Milton Meltzer, Diane Stanley, Jerry Stanley.
Adamson, Lynda G. *American Historical Fiction: An Annotated Guide to Novels for Adults and Young Adults.* Phoenix: Oryx Press, 1999.

Adamson, Lynda G. *Recreating the Past: A Guide to American and World Historical Fiction for Children and Young Adults*. Westport, Connecticut: Greenwood Press, 1994.

Adamson, Lynda G. *World Historical Fiction: An Annotated Guide to Novels for Adults and Young Adults*. Phoenix: Oryx Press, 1999.

Emerson, Kathy Lynn. *The Writer's Guide to Everyday Life in Renaissance England*. Cincinnati: Writers Digest Books, 1996

Hughes, Kristine. *The Writer's Guide to Everyday Life in Regency and Victorian England*. Cincinnati: Writers Digest Books, 1998.

Kenyon, Sherrilyn. *Everyday Life in the Middle Ages*. Cincinnati: Writers Digest Books, 1995.

McCutcheon, Marc. *Everyday Life in the 1800's*. Cincinnati: Writers Digest Books, 2001.

Moulton, Candy Vyvey. *The Writer's Guide to Everyday Life in the Wild West*. Cincinnati: Writers Digest Books, 1999.

Taylor, Dale. *Writer's Guide to Everyday Life in Colonial America*. Cincinnati: Writers Digest Books, 1999.

Varhola, Michael J. *The Writer's Guide to Everyday Life During the Civil War*. Cincinnati: Writer's Digest Books, 1999.

World Book Encyclopedia. Chicago: World Book, Inc., 2001.

Electronic

"American History." Harker Heights—Kileen—World Connections. 9 July 2001 <http://killeenroos.com/link/amhist.htm>.

"American Memory." Library of Congress. 1 June 2001. 9 July 2001 <http://memory.loc.gov/>.

EyeWitness: History Through the Eyes of Those Who Lived It. 9 July 2001. 9 July 2001 <http://www.ibiscom.com/>.

Primary Search Online. EBSCO Publishing. Requires subscription.

"Primary Sources and Activities." *National Archives and Records Administration*. 2 Jan. 2001 1 February 2002 <http://www.nara.gov/education/teaching/teaching.html>.

Product or Culminating Activity: History Fair—Open to all other students, parents, and community members.

Assessment Overview: The classroom teacher uses rubrics for the book report and research paper. No summative information literacy assessment is given other than what is implicitly embedded in their research. However, the primary focus for the librarian is on formative assessment. It is important that each student learn how to organize his/her searches independently. The History Fair Research Worksheet gives them a "framework" for how to proceed, and it allows the LMS and teacher to see at a glance where problems might arise.

Figure 4.46 **History Fair**

Research Planner

Name _____

Historical Fiction Title _____

Time period _____

Major Events:

Your Questions:

Initial Keywords:	New Keywords:

Places that you have checked (Use keywords above; add new ones as you find them):

_____ Card catalog/online library catalog
_____ Noted OTHER keywords or subject headings from the tracings on the entry
_____ Located books found with catalog search
      _____ used book index   _____ used book's table of contents
_____ *World Book Encyclopedia*
_____ Historical encyclopedia
_____ Books of chronology
_____ Magazine Index(es) (which ones?) _____ _____
      _____ Located articles found with index search
_____ Vertical File (what headings did you check?)

When you have exhausted the above resources, you might wish to pursue the following options.
_____ Internet Research
_____ Began search with directory like Yahoo or search engine like Alta Vista
      _____ What keywords did you use? _____ _____
      _____ *In general*, what were the results of your search?
            _____ Too many "hits"? (Try narrowing your search terms)
            _____ Too few "hits"? (Try making your search term broader)
_____ Local historical society
_____ Individual who lived during this time period

Figure 4.47 **History Fair**

Book Report Rubric

Paragraph • main idea • characters • time period • location • story evaluation	**Poor**	**Fair**	**Good**	**Excellent**
Four things learned about time period/details	**Poor**	**Fair**	**Good**	**Excellent**
Grammar • good sentences • paragraphs • punctuation • spelling	**Poor**	**Fair**	**Good**	**Excellent**
Appearance • neatly done • easy for others to read	**Poor**	**Fair**	**Good**	**Excellent**

Figure 4.48   **History Fair**

Research Paper Product Descriptor

Parts	Points		Attributes
	Self Assessment	**Teacher Assessment**	
Title Page	_____	_____	**Elements** • Illustration depicting topic • Title of paper in bold • Name/Date • Teacher's name
Note Card	_____	_____	Complete • Organized and labeled
Body of Paper	_____	_____	Explains info in own words • Accurate • Factual • Describes important areas • Organized into paragraphs • Complete • Includes a CONCLUSION explaining what you learned from this assignment
Mechanics	_____	_____	Organized paragraphs • Correct grammar, spelling, capitals, & punctuation • Complete and interesting sentences • Margins • Indented
Bibliography	_____	_____	Followed guidelines • Sources in ABC order
Other	_____	_____	
		_____	◀ **Your Average Score**

Student Comments	Teacher Comments

If These Walls Could Speak

Ronda Hassig, Library Media Specialist
Janet Barnett, Former Communication Arts/Social Studies/Reading Teacher
Harmony Middle School
10101 West 141st St., Overland Park, KS 66221
913-681-4819
hassig@hotmail.com

Grade Level: 6

Unit Overview: If These Walls Could Speak integrates information skills with two of the four core units of study. In communications arts, students will read a novel, *Randall's Wall* by Carol Fenner, which examines emotional walls, and will also read designated easy books containing emotional walls and biases. In social studies, students will use listening, map, charting, and research skills surrounding physical walls and will read the book *Talking Walls* by Margy Burns Knight, illustrated by Anne Sibley O'Brien.

Time Frame: No more than five class days in the library
Scheduling Note: The unit is predicated on an intricate pattern of library use. Initially two groups use the library. One group of at least 16 students undertakes matching, charting, and mapping for approximately an hour and a half. The second group of up to 25 students reads for two to three hours. (Students can also come back repeatedly to read when they aren't in the other two groups.) After the first group completes their work, a third group uses the library for research, which can take up to three hours. Depending on the size of the team, rotation through all of the stations can take up to a week.

Content Area Standards: Blue Valley School District Standards, Overland Park, Kansas

Communication Arts, Grades 6–8

Listening Outcome: The student will demonstrate effective listening skills in both formal and informal situations.
Benchmark 1: The student will understand listening strategies necessary to construct meaning in a variety of situations, as described by the following indicators:
1.1. Demonstrate active listening by restating, responding, summarizing and asking clarifying questions about what was heard.
1.4. Practice proper listening etiquette in group settings.

Reading Outcome: The student will construct meaning from a variety of materials.
Benchmark 2: The student will read a variety of texts and genres to construct meaning and to make thoughtful connections, as described by the following indicators:
2.2. Identify topics and themes from a variety of sources to make connections from reading.
2.3. Demonstrate ability to self-assess and reflect on own reading.

2.11. Begin to analyze, interpret, draw conclusions and question literary elements in technical writing and other nonfiction texts. e.g., organization and structure, author's purpose, main idea, supporting details and audience.

Life Skills Outcome: The student will demonstrate necessary life skills to work effectively and with integrity in groups and independently for a variety of purposes.

Benchmark 4: The student will demonstrate effective life skills through integrated activities within individual and group settings, as described by the following indicators:

4.2. Contribute and behave appropriately in both small and large groups.

4.4. Manage time and materials effectively.

4.5. Demonstrate organizational skills during independent and group time.

Information-Processing Outcome: The student will demonstrate skills for accessing, processing and synthesizing information.

Benchmark 7: The student will access, process, integrate and evaluate information using a variety of sources, as described by the following indicators:

7.1. Define the problem, determine prior knowledge, narrow the topic and identify the information needed.

7.2. Seek information from all possible sources and select the most appropriate source.

7.3. Locate and extract relevant information from within sources.

7.5. Synthesize information from multiple sources and present the research, citing resources.

Social Studies Curriculum, Grade 6

Outcome 3: Geography. The sixth grade student will use geographic concepts and skills to describe human behavior in ancient and medieval societies and the contemporary world.

6.5 Use essential map skills including scale, directional indicators, symbols, legends, latitude and longitude.

Information Power Information Literacy Standards and Indicators: 1.1, 1.4, 1.5, 2.1, 2.4, 3.1, 3.2, 3.3, 3.4, 5.1, 5.2, 6.2, 7.2, 9.1, 9.2

Cooperative Teaching Plan:

Library Media Specialist Will:

- Arrange the library media center in two areas. One side will house tables containing the easy books that students will Read and Chart, Read and Respond to, and Just Read. The other side will house four tables, each with four pictures of different physical walls and four cards with one fact about one of the walls, for a total of sixteen cards at each table. Four students will sit at each table.
- Assist students at each table as they match the four facts with the corresponding wall.
- Direct students in their creation of a wall chart while reading *Talking Walls*.
- Help table groups to locate walls in atlases and mark them on large blank world maps.
- Advise individual students as they locate all countries on personal size world maps.
- Assist individual students as they choose a wall and answer questions about its location using an atlas, *CultureGrams*, *Lands and Peoples*, and the *World Almanac*.
- Help students as they complete their KWL activity on their wall, writing five facts they know, five facts they want to know, and finally three paragraphs on what they learned.
- Assess the social studies component.

Classroom Teacher Will:

- Teach atlas skills in preparation for table activity.
- Teach bibliographic citation skills for the sources used in individual wall research.
- Teach students the meaning of bias.
- Supervise students in reading the easy books and recording them in their literature logs.
- Assess literature logs.
- Undertake a study of the novel *Randall's Wall* by Carol Fenner.
- Read and assess *Randall's Wall* assessment activities.

Resources:

Print

Allan, Nicholas. *The Hefty Fairy*. New York: Arrow, 1989.

Allen, Judy. *What is a Wall, After All?* Cambridge, Massachusetts: Candlewick, 1993.

Cohen, Barbara. *Molly's Pilgrim*. New York: Lothrop, Lee & Shepard, 1983.

Cohen, Miriam. *No Good in Art*. New York: Morrow, 1980.

CultureGrams. Orem, Utah: CultureGrams, 2001.

DePaola, Tomie. *Oliver Button is a Sissy*. New York: Harcourt, 1979.

Dugan, Barbara. *Loop the Loop*. New York: Greenwillow, 1992.

Ernst, Lisa Campbell. *Sam Johnson and the Blue Ribbon Quilt*. New York: HarperCollins, 1985.

Fenner, Carol. *Randall's Wall*. New York: Simon and Schuster, 1991.

Haggerty, Mary Elizabeth. *A Crack in the Wall*. New York: Lee & Low, 1993.

Henkes, Kevin. *Chrysanthemum*. New York: HarperCollins, 1991.

Innocenti, Roberto. *Rose Blanche*. San Diego: Harcourt, 1996.

Knight, Margy Burns. *Talking Walls*. Gardiner, Maine: Tilbury House, 1992.

Lands and Peoples. Danbury, Connecticut: Grolier, Inc., 2001.

Lasker, Joe. *Nick Joins In*. Chicago: Whitman, 1980.

Lionni, Leo. *Tillie and the Wall*. New York: Knopf, 1989.

Mills, Lauren. *The Rag Coat*. Boston: Little, Brown & Company, 1991.

Mochizuki, Ken. *Baseball Saved Us*. New York: Lee & Low, 1993.

Monk, Lorraine. *Photographs that Changed the World*. New York: Doubleday, 1989.

Schotter, Roni. *Captain Snap and the Children of Vinegar Lane*. New York: Orchard, 1989.

O'Shaughnessy, Ellen Cassels. *Somebody Called Me a Retard Today—And My Heart Felt Sad*. New York: Walker, 1992.

Uchida, Yoshiko. *The Bracelet*. New York: Philomel, 1993.

World Almanac and Book of Facts. Cleveland, Ohio: World Almanac Education, 2001.

Electronic

Talking Walls. CD-ROM. Redmond, Washington: Edmark, 1999.

Talking Walls: The Stories Continue. CD-ROM. Redmond, Washington: Edmark, 2000.

Supplies

Laminated pictures of each physical wall

Four facts on large index cards on each wall

Large laminated world maps without country names

Small individual world maps without country names

Large plastic bags to hold easy book and response card

Product or Culminating Activity: Students produce a Wall Chart, Wall Map, and KWL for the Social Studies component. They log all of their easy reading and bias work for the Communication Arts component in addition to reading *Randall's Wall* by Carol Fenner. As a culminating event, a counselor comes to talk to students about emotional walls. Students can also act out emotional walls.

Assessment Overview: In social studies, students are assessed on their map skills—using an atlas to correctly place a wall's location on a world map. On all written work, students are assessed on spelling and legibility. The KWL requires accuracy of information and citation of sources for the research portion. The LMS assesses this component. Students complete the *Randall's Wall* assessment activities. All assessments are done using a traditional read and respond grading method without rubrics.

Adaptations and Extensions: This unit can be adapted in many ways. Extending the requirements for research, using fewer or more walls, and adding the math and science components are just a few possibilities. In math, students might learn about positive and negative space. In science students might build dams. Sixth grade, with its study of ancient civilizations, lends itself well to this unit. However, seventh grade world geography is also compatible with this unit. If the teachers have any artifacts for the social studies component, they should be used (e.g., a video recording of the Berlin Wall going up or coming down or an actual piece of the Berlin Wall for students to touch).

Figure 4.49   **If These Walls Could Speak**

Easy Reading List

Read and Chart

_____ Allan, Nicholas. *The Hefty Fairy*.

_____ DePaola, Tomie. *Oliver Button Is a Sissy*.

_____ Cohen, Barbara. *Molly's Pilgrim*.

_____ Henkes, Kevin. *Chrysanthemum*.

_____ Ernst, Lisa Campbell. *Sam Johnson and the Blue Ribbon Quilt*.

Read and Respond

_____ Allen, Judy. *What Is a Wall, After All?*

_____ Uchida, Yoshiko. *The Bracelet*.

_____ Mochizuki, Ken. *Baseball Saved Us*.

_____ Lionni, Leo. *Tillie and the Wall*.

_____ Innocenti, Roberto. *Rose Blanche*.

_____ Mills, Lauren. *The Rag Coat*.

_____ O'Shaughnessy, Ellen Cassels. *Somebody Called Me a Retard Today...And My Heart Felt Sad*.

Read

_____ Lasker, Joe. *Nick Joins In*.

_____ Dugan, Barbara. *Loop the Loop*.

_____ Cohen, Miriam. *No Good in Art*.

_____ Haggerty, Mary Elizabeth. *A Crack in the Wall*.

_____ Schotter, Roni. *Captain Snap and the Children of Vinegar Lane*.

Figure 4.50 **If These Walls Could Speak**

Read and Chart

Read the books in the "Read and Chart" section and chart this information about each:

Title:

Author:

Main Character(s):

Bias:

Personal Response:

Figure 4.51   **If These Walls Could Speak**

Read and Respond
(Sample)

Open Read and Respond book bag, read the book, read the response card, and then answer the questions asked in your Literature journal:

Author: Leo Lionni

Title: *Tillie and the Wall*

What's interesting about the celebration pebble?

What's the *moral* of this story?

Why is Tillie a hero?

Is the wall in this book emotional or physical or both? Explain.

Figure 4.52 **If These Walls Could Speak**

Additional Read and Respond Question Sets

Rose Blanche **by Roberto Innocenti**

1. Read the text.

2. How did this story make you feel?

3. Turn to page 27 of *Photographs That Changed the World* by Lorraine Monk. Read the message with the picture.

4. Find a similar picture in Rose Blanche.

5. Answer: Who? What? When? Where? Why? And how does it relate to the present?

Somebody Called Me a Retard Today...and My Heart Felt Sad **by Ellen O'Shaughnessy**

1. Read the story.

2. In your literature log write the title and author.

   a. How did the text make you feel?

   b. Write about a time someone called you a name and you felt badly.

   c. What do you do when people start name-calling?

   d. List 10 ways to get others to stop calling people names.

The Rag Coat **by Lauren Mills**

1. Read the text.

2. In your literature log, write about the discrimination you see in this book.

The Bracelet **by Yoshiko Uchida and** *Baseball Saved Us* **by Ken Mochizuki**

1. Read both books.

2. In your literature log write titles, authors, and what you remember from reading these two books.

3. What do these children suffer from in these two books? Explain.

4. How do they survive?

   Be sure to look through the attached book *Manzanar*.

What Is a Wall, After All? **by Judy Allen**

1. Read the book.

2. In your literature log write the title and author and what you remember from the book.

3. Reread. Look carefully—there's lots of information here.

4. List any new information.

Figure 4.53   **If These Walls Could Speak**

Randall's Wall Evaluation Activities

I. Discuss the following questions: (two pages)

- ■ What events occurred in the story that helped Randall tear down his wall?

- ■ Jean showed us in the story that one person really can make a difference. Discuss how you might be able to make a difference in someone's life.

II. Write a cinquain poem about Randall.
Use his name for the first line, two adjectives to describe him in the second line, three words to explain his wall in the third line, four words in the fourth line explaining what helped him tear down his wall, and one word in the fifth line that you think best describes how Randall felt at the end of the book. Publish your poem in ink or word process.

III. Make a collage of pictures and words.
Show the characteristics, traits, life skills, and talents of either Randall or Jean.

IV. Answer the following questions (Write at least ½ page response.)

- ■ Of all the activities we did with this novel, which one did you enjoy the most?

- ■ Which caused you to learn the most?

Figure 4.54 **If These Walls Could Speak**

List of Walls
(Sample)

- **Forbidden City**—China

- **The Western Wall**—Israel

- **Lascaux Cave**—France

- **Great Wall of China**—China

- **Kaaba**—Saudi Arabia

- **Great Zimbabwe Conical Towers**—Zimbabwe

- **Vietnam War Memorial**—Washington, D.C.

- **Nelson Mandela Prison Walls**—South Africa

- **Pyramids**—Egypt

- **Berlin Wall**—Germany

- **Hadrian's Wall**—England/Scotland

- **Inca Ruins**—Cuzco, Peru

- **Tower of London**—England

- **Krah des Chevaliers (Crusader Castle)**—Syria

- **The Vatican**—Vatican City

- **Stonehenge**—England

*Note: List can be adapted to align with current social studies topic.

Figure 4.55   If These Walls Could Speak

Physical Walls Research Questions

Answer these questions about the wall of your choice and the country in which it is located.

Name of wall: _____

Country in which the wall is located: _____

Using an Atlas
 1. What is the capital of this country?
 2. On what continent is your wall located?

Using an Almanac
 3. What is the population of this country?
 4. What is the monetary unit for this country?
 5. What is the literacy rate for this country?
 6. How many television sets per person are there in this country?
 7. What is the life expectancy for males and females in this country?

Using *CultureGrams*
 8. What is one way to say "Hello" in this country?
 9. Name a special eating habit in this country.
10. When can a young person begin dating in this country?
11. What is the official language of this country?
12. What do people do for recreation in this country?

Using *Lands and Peoples*
13. Besides the wall, what other places of interest might one visit in this country?
14. Name a mountain range in this country.
15. Name a famous river in this country.
16. Name a city in this country besides the capital.

Now consider these complex thinking questions. Choose one to answer in a complete, well-written paragraph on your chosen wall:

 1. In what way did or does your wall affect the world around it?
 2. Why has your wall lasted as long as it has?
 3. If your wall is an emotional wall explain why.
 4. If your wall is a political wall explain why.
 5. If your wall is in Great Britain or the Middle East, try to explain why there are so many walls located in these areas.

Figure 4.56 **If These Walls Could Speak**

Social Studies Requirements

Each student will be responsible to complete a packet including:
>Walls World Map
>Walls Chart
>Physical Walls Research Question Sheet
>Walls KWL

on a wall of his/her choice.

Research will be conducted in the Library Media Center.

Walls Chart

The class has 16 pictures of walls, 4 descriptive cards with each picture, 4 pictures to a table. In your table group, sort the cards and match the facts with the correct wall. Once everything is sorted correctly, the library media specialist will verify the correct identification of all walls and their locations.

Now create and complete the following chart for all 16 walls, your own 4 and the 12 from the other 3 groups:

Name of Wall	Location	Physical	Emotional	Political
Western Wall	Jerusalem, Israel	X	X	X

Walls Map

Each group will locate the countries in which their walls are located on the large world map. After the walls are all identified on the map, you will complete an individual world map for your packet including the location of all 16 walls (the 4 from your group and the 12 located by the other 3 groups).

KWL

On a separate sheet, complete a KWL on the wall of your choice. List at least five things for K (Know) and W (Want to know). Now write at least three paragraphs about L (what you Learned), relying on your research in the Library Media Center.

What do you Know?

What do you Want to know?

What did you Learn?

Is Listening Reading?

Toni Buzzeo, Library Media Specialist
Lori Carlson, Grade 5 Teacher
Longfellow Elementary School
432 Stevens Avenue, Portland, ME 04093
207-874-8195
tonibuzzeo@tonibuzzeo.com

Grade Level: 5

Unit Overview: Audiobooks are a popular mode of 'reading' among students in the intermediate grades. However, few have thought about the nature of this type of reading, or about the quality of the audiobook production and how it influences their experience of the book. Is Listening Reading? was designed by a library media specialist and classroom teacher to encourage students to hone their audiobook listening skills, to practice evaluation of the quality of audiobooks they 'read,' to learn to write and orally deliver an audiobook review, and to personally examine, publicly discuss, and write about the essential question, "Is listening reading?"

Time Frame: 4 weeks

Content Area Standards: Learning Results, Portland Public Schools, Portland, Maine
<http://www.portlandschools.org/Pages/Education/EducationFrame.html>

Language Arts, 3–5 (Level 2)
Standard I Reading: Uses reading skills and strategies to comprehend, interpret, and evaluate what is read.
I.1 Uses comprehension strategies to make sense of narrative texts.

Standard II Literature: Explores, experiences, selects, and understands literature from a variety of collections.
II.1 Reads and interprets literature from a variety of genres and formats;
II.2 Identifies and articulates personal reading preferences among genres and categories.

Standard III Writing: Uses the skills and strategies of the writing process for reflective, creative, and informational purposes.
III.1 Uses planning, drafting, and revising to produce a finished work;
III.2 Uses self-editing through proofreading and rereading, and seeks help from others to edit and improve writing;
III.3 Writes pieces that show awareness of a variety of intended audiences and identifiable purposes;
III.5 Writes expository pieces with a central idea and supporting details.

Standard IV Speaking and Listening: Demonstrates competence in speaking and listening as tools for learning.

IV.1 Contributes to a group discussion;

IV.3 Listens to classmates and adults without interrupting;

IV.4 Makes effort to have a clear main point when speaking to others.

Information Power Information Literacy Standards and Indicators: 1.1, 1.4, 1.5, 2.2, 2.4, 3.1, 3.2, 3.3, 3.4, 5.2, 9.1, 9.2, 9.3

Cooperative Teaching Plan:

Library Media Specialist Will:

- Introduce the discussion topic, "Is Listening Reading?" with the classroom teacher.
- Booktalk 30 audiobook titles from the collection.
- Create and introduce a list of audiobook reviewing guidelines.
- Introduce the concept of audiobook reviewing by sharing several audiobook reviews from past issues of AudioFile Magazine.
- Listen to and review an audiobook and write a review of it.
- Read rough drafts of student reviews and conference with students to suggest revisions.
- Assess student audiobook reviews using a rubric.
- Host an audiobook review session in which students deliver their audiobook reviews into a microphone for an audience of classmates.
- Deliver an oral audio review at the audiobook review session in the library media center.
- Host a roundtable discussion of the question, "Is Listening Reading?"
- Host a class reading of persuasive essays in the library media center.

Classroom Teacher Will:

- Introduce the discussion topic, "Is Listening Reading?" with the LMS.
- Post these questions in the classroom:
  - What is reading?
  - What new things are you discovering about reading by listening?
  - Are you reading the audiobook you are reviewing?
  - Is listening reading?
- Assign students to gather information about "reading" by using dictionaries, thesauri, and personal interviews.
- Listen to and review an audiobook and write a review of it.
- Read rough drafts of student reviews and conference with students to suggest revisions.
- Assess student audiobook reviews using a rubric.
- Deliver an oral audio review at the audiobook review session in the library media center.
- Prepare students for roundtable discussion of the question, "Is Listening Reading?"
- Teach students to write a five paragraph persuasive essay in which they argue that listening is or is not reading.
- Read rough drafts of student essays and conference with students to suggest revisions.
- Assess student essays using a rubric.

Resources:

Print

"Children, Young Adult, and Family Listening Audiobook Reviews." *AudioFile Magazine,* 1998–2002.

A variety of dictionaries and thesauri, including:

American Heritage Student Dictionary. Boston: Houghton Mifflin, 1998.

Bollard, John K. *Scholastic Children's Thesaurus.* New York: Scholastic, 1998.

Hellweg, Paul. *The American Heritage Children's Thesaurus.* Boston: Houghton Mifflin, 1997.

Macmillan Dictionary for Children. New York: Simon and Schuster, 1997.

Scholastic Children's Dictionary. New York: Scholastic, 1996.

World Book Dictionary. Chicago: World Book, Inc., 2000.

Electronic

"Current Reviews." *AudioFile.* 3 February 2002 <http://www.audiofilemagazine.com/reviews.html>.

Audiovisuals

A variety of unabridged audiobook recordings of middle grade fiction and nonfiction books.

Equipment

Portable microphone

Product or Culminating Activities: Students will write and orally deliver an audiobook review and a five paragraph persuasive essay. They will also participate in a round table discussion of the question: *Is Listening Reading?*

Assessment Overview:

The audiobook review is jointly assessed by the LMS and the teacher with a rubric. The five paragraph persuasive essay is assessed by the teacher with a rubric. Student participation in the roundtable discussion is assessed by the LMS and the teacher by the playing of a poker chip each time a student contributes to the discussion. (Each student must make at least one point. No one may use more than three chips until everyone has spoken at least once.)

Figure 4.57 **Is Listening Reading?**

Audiobook Reviewing Guidelines

■ Your audiobook review must be between 110 and 120 words long.

■ Make every review UNIQUE (your "voice," vocabulary, way of telling).

■ You are not reviewing the BOOK (no opinions about only the book).

■ You are reviewing the AUDIORECORDING of the book.

■ Give as many specifics as possible about HOW and WHY the audiorecording is successful (or is not successful).

■ Pay attention to:

　　Narrative voice and style (such as pace)

　　Vocal characterization (changing voices for different characters)

　　Enhancement of the text (music, sound effects)

　　Do these elements work well or not?

■ Summarize the plot quickly (in 2-3 sentences) and get on with the review!

Figure 4.58   Is Listening Reading?

Audiobook Reviewing Rubric

Student _____

Evaluator _____

	Distinguished	Advanced	Basic	Novice
Review meets length guidelines.	4	3	2	1
Review is properly formatted.	4	3	2	1
Review includes the author and title of the book and the name of the narrator.	4	3	2	1
Student's individual "voice," vocabulary, and personality are evident.	4	3	2	1
Review clearly focuses on quality of audiorecording rather than book quality.	4	3	2	1
The plot is efficiently summarized in two or three sentences.	4	3	2	1
Review includes specifics on:				
Narrative voice and style	4	3	2	1
Vocal characterizations	4	3	2	1
Enhancement of the text (music, sound effects)	4	3	2	1
Finished copy exhibits grade appropriate mechanics.	4	3	2	1

Comments:

Figure 4.59   Is Listening Reading?

Audiobooks: Listening , Reading, or Both?
Essay Guidelines

Construct an essay explaining whether you believe listening to an audiobook is or is not reading. Follow the Constructing Support essay format you have worked on all year, which includes:

1. Introductory paragraph stating your opinion and purpose (to convince or explain);

2. At least three supporting paragraphs—each paragraph clearly stating and developing a support/reason;

3. A concluding paragraph in which you restate your position.

Somewhere in your essay you must include:

1. A text definition of reading;

2. The opinion of someone you surveyed either as a direct or an indirect quote.

Figure 4.60 | **Is Listening Reading?**

Audiobooks: Listening, Reading, or Both?
Essay Rubric

Student _____

Evaluator _____

Essay Parts	Exceeds Standards	Meets Standards	Does Not Meet Standards
Introduction	Clearly states position and purpose in an interesting, detailed way	States position and purpose	No statement of position and/or purpose
Paragraphs	Each paragraph has clearly stated main idea and reasons supported with examples	Each paragraph has main idea and reasons	Paragraphs have no clearly definable main idea
Definition of Reading	Clearly stated definition of reading which enhances the argument in the text	Definition of reading is included in at least one passage	No definition of reading is included
Quote	Direct or indirect quote from surveyed person enhances the argument	Direct or indirect quote is included	No incorporation of direct or indirect quote in the text
Mechanics	Exceeds grade level expectations	Meets grade level expectations	Below grade level expectations

Lions, Tigers, and Bears!
Jill Brown, Library Media Specialist
Margaret Clonan, Grade 3 Teacher; Colleen Zimmerman, Technology Coordinator
Nardin Academy
135 Cleveland Ave., Buffalo, NY 14222
716-881-6262
buflib@yahoo.com

Grade Level: 3

Unit Overview: In Lions, Tigers, and Bears! third grade students research the habitat, food, and means of protection for selected animals. They learn to locate and use a variety of information sources, write a bibliography, take notes using cards, organize, and write a research report.

Time Frame: Yearlong project. (Third grade is the only grade that, due to space and personnel limitations, has weekly scheduled library periods.)

Content Area Standards: New York State Learning Standards
<http://www.nysatl.nysed.gov/standards.html>

Mathematics, Science and Technology, Elementary
Standard 2. Information Systems: Students will access, generate, and transfer information using appropriate technologies.
Indicator. Access needed information from printed media, electronic databases, and community resources.

Standard 4. Science: Students will understand and apply scientific concepts, principles, and theories to the physical setting and living environment and recognize the historical development of ideas of science.
Indicator. The Living Environment. Describe the life processes common to all living things.
Indicator. The Living Environment. Describe some survival behaviors of common living specimens

English Language Arts, Elementary
Standard 3. Language for Critical Analysis and Evaluation: Students will listen, speak, read, and write for critical analysis and evaluation. As listeners and readers, students will analyze experiences, ideas, information, and issues presented by others using a variety of established criteria. As speakers and writers, they will use oral and written language that follows the accepted conventions of the English language to present, from a variety of perspectives, their opinions and judgments on experiences, ideas, information, and issues.
Indicator. Speaking and Writing. Monitor and adjust their own oral and written presentations to meet criteria for competent performance (e.g., in writing, the criteria might include development of position, organization, appropriate vocabulary, mechanics, and neatness. In speaking, the criteria might include good content, effective delivery, diction, posture, poise, and eye contact)

Information Power Information Literacy Standards and Indicators: 1.1, 1.2, 1.3, 1.4, 1.5, 2.1, 2.2, 2.3, 2.4, 3.1, 3.2, 3.3, 3.4, 6.1, 6.2, 7.1, 7.2, 6.1, 8.2, 8.3

Cooperative Teaching Plan:

Library Media Specialist Will:
- ◼ Teach students a research model to be followed for this and all research projects
  - What do I need to know?
  - What will I do with the information?
  - What words and phrases can I use to look up information?
  - What are likely sources of information?
  - Write out bibliographic information.
  - Take notes on cards—one fact per card.
  - Organize, write, and edit final product.
  - Introduce resources most useful for the project and teach location and use of them.
  - Review animal selections to eliminate those animals for which the library has insufficient information.
  - Assist with research, bibliography format, and note taking, all of which happen during school hours (although students are encouraged to bring available sources from home).

Classroom Teacher Will:
- ◼ Assign and explain project.
- ◼ Teach bibliography format and note taking using cards—one fact per card.
- ◼ Assist with use of resources.
- ◼ Teach organizing of information, writing, and editing.
- ◼ Assess the printed booklet using a rubric.

Technology Coordinator Will:
- ◼ Teach word processing and assist with word processing of the final project.

Resources:

Print
Amazing Animals of the World. Danbury, Connecticut: Grolier, 1995.
Animal Fact File Cards Danbury, Connecticut: Grolier, 1967.
Ranger Rick. Reston, Virginia: National Wildlife Federation.
Wildlife and Plants of the World. New York: Marshall Cavendish, 1999.
World Book Student Discovery Encyclopedia. Chicago: World Book, Inc., 2000.
Zoobooks Magazine. Poway, California: Wildlife Education, Ltd.

Electronic
"Kratt's Creatures." PBS. 11 July 2001 <http://www.pbs.org/kratts>.
Sea World/Busch Gardens Animal Information Database. 11 July 2001 <http://www.seaworld.org>.
SIRS Discoverer (Full text online database—requires subscription)
St. Louis Zoo. 11 July 2001 <http://www.stlzoo.org>.

Product or Culminating Activity: Students produce a written report. Classroom teacher assesses printed booklet using the rubric. The booklets are displayed in the hallway outside the classroom with comment sheets attached for students, parents, other teachers, and others to use.

Assessment Overview: Student products are assessed using a rubric with the following standard grading scale for primary grade products: E—excellent G—good P—passing N—not passing

Figure 4.61   **Lions, Tigers, and Bears!**

Research Model

1. What information do I need?

    ■ Where does my animal live?
    ■ What does it eat?
    ■ How does it protect itself?

2. What am I going to do with this information?

    ■ Make a booklet using Writing Center (word processing program).
    ■ Cover should include your name as well as the name and a picture of your animal.
    ■ Introduction page stating why you chose this animal.
    ■ One page for each topic—habitat, food, and protection—with picture for each.
    ■ Final page should list all the sources you used in alphabetical order.

3. What words and phrases can I use to look up information on my topic?

    ■ Specific animal name
    ■ Type of animal (e.g., mammal, bird, insect)
    ■ Place it lives (e.g., Australia, jungles)

4. What resources are likely to have the information I need?

    ■ Books about animals
    ■ Encyclopedias
    ■ Magazines
    ■ Internet
    ■ *Animal Fact File Cards*

    ■ You must use a variety of sources.
    ■ You must have at least 2 sources for each topic.

5. Write down bibliographic information. Take notes.

    ■ Use sample cards for reference.

6. Write your report. Read it over and rewrite if necessary. Correct mistakes. Make your cover. Select pictures to go with each section.

7. Have fun!

Figure 4.62   Lions, Tigers, and Bears!

Assessment Tool

Name _____   Grade _____

	Possible Points	Score

A. Note cards with complete sources listed
   at the bottom   25   _____

B. Written report from notes, listing sources

   Habitat   15   _____

   Food   15   _____

   Protection   15   _____

C. Typed report and bibliography   15   _____

D. Report booklet including pictures to
   illustrate the cover and each section   15   _____

                                              TOTAL   _____

Marking Code
E   Excellent   = 98–100 points
G   Good   = 90–97   points
P   Passing   = 80–89   points
N   Not Passing   = 79 or fewer points

PLEASE DETACH AND RETURN TO TEACHER

My signature below indicates that I have received my child's research report.

_____

Student Name

_____

Parent Signature

Medieval Magic
Deborah A. Monck, Media Specialist
Holly Thompson, Nancy Johnson, Kaye Carpenter, Cheryl Vollmar, Michelle Taylor, Grade 3 Teachers
Meadow Park Elementary School
3131 Lakeview Boulevard, Port Charlotte, FL 33948
941-255-7470
monckstr@sunline.net

Grade Level: 3

Unit Overview: Medieval Magic, an interdisciplinary study of the medieval period, emphasizes information literacy skills in the media center that integrate social studies content taught in the classroom. In the media center, small class groups rotate through six learning centers to review library skills (encyclopedia, thesaurus, dictionary and Dewey Decimal), allow free browsing of medieval fiction and nonfiction titles, and encourage creativity in a bookmark making activity. All classes enjoy an enthusiastic reading of *The Knight Who Was Afraid of the Dark* with illustrations projected on a large screen in the media center.

Time Frame: 3 weeks on a fixed library schedule

Content Area Standards: Florida Sunshine State Standards <http://www.firn.edu/doe/menu/sss.htm>

Social Studies, Grades 3–5

Strand A. Time, Continuity, and Change (History)
Standard 1: The learner understands historical chronology and the historical perspective.
SS.A.1.2.1: The learner understands how individuals, ideas, decisions, and events can influence history.
SS.A.1.2.3: The learner understands broad categories of time in years, decades, and centuries.

Standard 2: The learner understands the world from its beginnings to the time of the Renaissance.
SS.A.2.2.1: The learner knows the significant scientific and technological achievements of various societies; e.g. the invention of paper in China, Mayan calendars, mummification, and the use of cotton in Egypt, astronomical discoveries in the Moslem world, and the Arabic number system.
SS.A.2.2.3: The learner understands various aspects of family life, structures, and roles in different cultures and in many eras; e.g. pastoral and agrarian families of early civilizations, families of ancient times, and medieval families.
SS.A.2.2.4: The learner understands the emergence of different laws and systems of government; e.g. monarchy and republic.
SS.A.2.2.5: The learner understands significant achievements in the humanities to the time of the Renaissance; e.g. Roman architecture and Greek art.

SS.A.2.2.7: The learner understands how developments in the Middle Ages contributed to modern life; e.g. the development of social institutions and organizations, the rise of cities, the formation of guilds, the rise of commerce, the influence of the church, and the rise of universities.

Information Power Information Literacy Standards and Indicators: 1.4, 3.1, 3.3, 6.1, 9.1, 9.3

Cooperative Teaching Plan

Library Media Specialist Will:
- Meet with classroom teachers to plan and implement unit.
- Provide library resources and materials for use in classroom instruction.
- Review previously taught encyclopedia, dictionary, thesaurus, and Dewey Decimal skills.
- Develop, facilitate, and evaluate learning centers, which will reinforce above skills.
- Present *The Knight Who Was Afraid of the Dark*, by Barbara Hazen, to entire third grade utilizing a camcorder, video projector, and large screen in the media center.

Teachers Will:
- Meet with LMS to plan and implement unit.
- Cover academic objectives and meet state content area standards.
- Collaborate with LMS to collect appropriate materials and resources.
- Allow adequate time in media center to review library skills (encyclopedia, dictionary, thesaurus, and Dewey Decimal) previously taught.
- Schedule class time in the media center to engage in centers and storytime.

Resources:

Print
Aliki. *A Medieval Feast.* New York: Crowell, 1983.

Bailey, Linda. *Adventures in the Middle Ages.* Toronto: Kids Can Press, 2000.

Blackwood, Gary. *Life in a Medieval Castle.* San Diego, CA: Lucent Books, 2000.

Czarnota, Lorna. *Medieval Tales That Kids Can Read and Tell.* Little Rock, AK: August House, 2000.

DK Merriam-Webster Children's Dictionary. New York: DK Publishing, 2000.

Gravett, Christopher. *Castle.* London: Dorling Kindersley, 2000.

Gravett, Christopher. *Knight.* London: Dorling Kindersley, 2000.

Hart, Avery. *Knights & Castles: 50 Hands-on Activities to Experience the Middle Ages.* Charlotte, VT: Williamson, 1998.

Hazen, Barbara Shook. *The Knight Who Was Afraid of the Dark.* New York: Puffin, 1992.

Hicks, Peter. *How Castles Were Built.* Austin, TX: Raintree Steck-Vaughn, 1999.

Langley, Andrew. *Medieval Life.* London: Dorling Kindersley, 2000.

Macauley, David. *Castle.* Boston: Houghton Mifflin, 1977.

MacDonald, Fiona. *A Medieval Castle.* New York: Peter Bedrick Books, 1990.

Maynard, Christopher. *Days of the Knights: A Tale of Castles and Battles.* New York: Dorling Kindersley, 1998.

The Middle Ages: A Watts Guide for Children. New York: Franklin Watts, 1999.

Reinagle, Damon. *Draw! Medieval Fantasies.* Columbus, NC: Peel Productions, 1995.

Scholastic Children's Thesaurus. New York: Scholastic, 1998.

Scieszka, Jon. *Knights of the Kitchen Table*. New York: Viking, 1991.

Skurzynski, Gloria. *The Minstrel in the Tower*. New York: Random House, 1988.

Steele, Philip. *Knights*. New York: Kingfisher, 1998.

World Book Encyclopedia. Chicago: World Book, Inc., 2001.

Electronic

Castles on the Web. 20 July 2001 <http://www.castlesontheweb.com/>.

Equipment

Camcorder

Video projector

Large projection screen

Product or Culminating Activity: Response sheets at centers with self-read instruction sheets and Dewey Decimal cards (20 cards numbered on back for self-checking) to be scrambled and put in Dewey order

Assessment Overview: Self-checking Dewey Decimal cards are numbered on the back. When students complete the process, they turn the cards over to check for proper numerical order. The library media specialist quickly assesses whether students have mastered the task. Completed response sheets at the centers are quickly assessed by the library media specialist using a rubric.

Figure 4.63   *Medieval Magic*

Encyclopedia Magic

Name_____

Teacher_____

Use the encyclopedias to look up the following medieval terms in bold. Browse articles and pictures for information. On the blank line, write the name of a **MODERN** term that is like the medieval word. In the box to the right, list traits that they have in common.

Knight _____

Castle _____

Jester _____

King _____

Wizard _____

Figure 4.64   **Medieval Magic**

Dewey Decimal Magic

Shuffle Dewey Cards.

■ Working as a group, put the cards in Dewey decimal order.

■ Check your work. There is a clue on the back.

■ Shuffle Dewey cards for the next group.

SAMPLES OF DEWEY DECIMAL MAGIC CARDS:

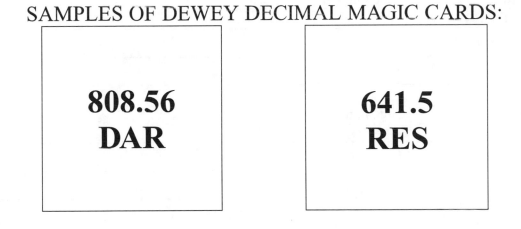

808.56
DAR

641.5
RES

Figure 4.65 **Medieval Magic**

Dictionary Dragons

Name _____

Teacher _____

_____

■ Please look up the following words in the dictionary. Don't forget to use the guide words at the top of the pages to help you find the words.

■ Write down the page number on which you find the word.

■ Write down the one sentence definition.

Knight   Page number _____
Definition: _____

_____

_____

Armor   Page number _____
Definition: _____

_____

_____

Joust   Page number _____
Definition: _____

_____

_____

Manor   Page number _____
Definition: _____

_____

_____

NEXT:
- Take a piece of manila art paper.
- Draw a medieval scene using ALL of the above words.
- Write the definitions around the edges of the paper.

Figure 4.66   **Medieval Magic**

BOOKMARK Magic

- Take one blank bookmark.

- Put your name and your teacher's name on the back.

- Design and color a medieval bookmark using one fact about medieval times that you've learned.

- Determine what the Dewey Decimal Number would be for the main picture in your bookmark and place that number on the bottom of your bookmark.

- Place finished bookmark in basket. We will be sharing them with all of the third grade classes – you will be receiving another third grader's design!

Figure 4.67 **Medieval Magic**

WORDS FIT FOR A KING

- Write your name in the rectangle on the top of the shield.

- Use the thesaurus to look up the words on the right side of the shield. Write down one synonym (word that means the same) for each of the words listed.

- Color your shield as you like.

Royal _____

Quest _____

Ruler _____

Knight _____

Figure 4.68 **Medieval Magic**

Assessment Rubric: Student Center Work

Expectations	Exceeds 3	Meets 2	Needs More Work 1	Score
Follows directions				
Listens to others				
Uses time wisely				
Grasps concept on response sheet				
Gives correct answers				
Completes work neatly				
Completes task on time				

Music and the Media Center

Ann van der Meulen, Library Media Specialist
Richard Coluzzi, Music Teacher
West Street Elementary School
30 West St., Geneva, NY 14456
315-781-4159 or 315-781-0406
avandermeulen@wfmail.genevacsd.org

Grade Level: 5

Unit Overview: In Music and the Media Center, students apply information retrieval skills to find answers to music-related questions posed by their music teacher. In groups, students rotate tasks, some in the music room, some in the library media center. Flexible scheduling affords students other opportunities to complete their library research as well. Students use a variety of information retrieval skills in an authentic point-of-need inquiry generated by a somewhat unlikely source—their music teacher.

Time Frame: Approximately one month

Content Area Standards: New York State Learning Standards
   < http://www.nysatl.nysed.gov/standards.html>

The Arts (specifically Music), Elementary:
Standard 1. Creating, Performing, and Participating in the Arts: Students will actively engage in the processes that constitute creation and performance in the arts (dance, music, theatre, and visual arts) and participate in various roles in the arts.
Indicator. Sing songs and play instruments, maintaining tone quality, pitch, rhythm, tempo, and dynamics; perform the music expressively; and sing or play simple repeated patterns (ostinatos) with familiar songs, rounds, partner songs, and harmonizing parts.
Standard 2. Knowing and Using Arts Materials and Resources: Students will be knowledgeable about and make use of the materials and resources available for participation in the arts in various roles.
Indicator. Use classroom and nontraditional instruments in performing and creating music.

English Language Arts, Elementary:
Standard 1. Language for Information and Understanding: Students will listen, speak, read, and write for information and understanding. As listeners and readers, students will collect data, facts, and ideas; discover relationships, concepts, and generalizations; and use knowledge generated from oral, written, and electronically produced texts. As speakers and writers, they will use oral and written language that follows the accepted conventions of the English language to acquire, interpret, apply, and transmit information.
Indicator. Gather and interpret information from children's reference books, magazines, textbooks, electronic bulletin boards, audio and media presentations, oral interviews, and from such forms as charts, graphs, maps, and diagrams.

Indicator. Select information appropriate to the purpose of their investigation and relate ideas from one text to another.

Indicator. Select and use strategies they have been taught for note taking, organizing, and categorizing information.

Indicator. Ask specific questions to clarify and extend meaning.

Indicator. Make appropriate and effective use of strategies to construct meaning from print, such as prior knowledge about a subject, structural and context clues, and an understanding of letter-sound relationships to decode difficult words.

Indicator. Include relevant information and exclude extraneous material.

Mathematics, Science and Technology, Elementary:

Standard 2. Information Systems: Students will access, generate, process, and transfer information using appropriate technologies.

Indicator: Access needed information from printed media, electronic data bases, and community resources.

Indicator: Demonstrate ability to evaluate information.

Information Power Information Literacy Standards and Indicators: 1.1, 1.2, 1.3, 1.4, 1.5, 2.1, 2.2, 2.3, 2.4, 3.2, 3.3, 6.1, 8.2, 8.3, 9.1, 9.2, 9.3

Cooperative Teaching Plan:

Library Media Specialist Will:

■ Prepare students by the time they are in fifth grade with information retrieval skills adequate to accomplish requested tasks, including the ability to:
  • Understand the research task.
  • Determine appropriate resources for locating information.
  • Locate and access information.
  • Read and understand located information.
  • Utilize information to answer questions.

■ Review with or guide students about information resources and retrieval strategies that might be appropriate for their needs.

■ Provide blocks of time for groups to visit the library during their music class times.

■ Provide individual support/guidance as needed.

Classroom Teacher Will:

■ Design music-related question sheets for students with input from library media specialist.

■ Divide class into groups.

■ Rotate groups among various tasks.

■ Assign tasks for groups:
  • Group I finds answers to music-related questions using resources found in the library media center.
  • Group II completes question sheet in music room using a CD-ROM on musical instruments.
  • Group III applies previous classroom instruction in playing techniques, rhythm, and note-reading skills by reading music and playing a variety of string instruments in the music room.
  • Group IV enhances rhythmic development using lummi sticks accompanied by selected music in the music room.

Resources:

Print

Diagram Group: The Scribner Guide to Orchestral Instruments. New York: Charles Scribner's Sons, 1983.

Kingfisher Young People's Book of Music. New York: Larousse Kingfisher Chambers, 1996.

Krull, Kathleen. *Lives of the Musicians: Good Times, Bad Times (And What the Neighbors Thought)*. San Diego: Harcourt Brace, 1993.

Scholastic Children's Dictionary. New York: Scholastic, 1996.

Ventura, Piero. *Great Composers*. New York: Putman, 1989.

World Book Encyclopedia. Chicago: World Book, 2001.

Electronic

Microsoft Musical Instruments. CD-ROM. Redmond, Washington: Microsoft, 1992.

World Book Millennium 2000: Deluxe Edition. CD-ROM. Chicago: World Book, 2000.

World Book Online. <http://www.worldbookonline.com> Requires subscription.

Equipment

Headphones

Variety of string instruments (guitar, dulcimer, banjo, string and electric bass, autoharp, violin

Lummi sticks

CD or tape player

Product or Culminating Activity: Students demonstrate their understanding of the research process by determining appropriate resources, locating and accessing information, reading and understanding what they have found, and applying their findings to the assigned task: completion of the question sheets designed by their music teacher.

Assessment Overview: Level of student participation and student ability to utilize information are assessed by the library media specialist and music teacher through observation and from student written responses. (Note Assessment Checklist.) Because questions are designed over a range of thinking skills (some very basic, others requiring analysis or synthesis), students must use problem-solving skills, application of knowledge, reading for meaning, evaluation of resources, and determination of the best course to accomplish the task at hand. The assessment evaluates students accordingly.

Figure 4.69   **Music and the Media Center**

Helpful Hints for Locating Information in the Library Media Center: A Quick Student Review

Do you understand what you are supposed to do?

What resources will help you? (Underline what you might use today.)

Teacher	OPAC (Catalog)	Encyclopedia	CD-ROMs
Librarian	Books	Almanac	Internet
Parent	Magazines	Atlas	Experts

Other Specific
Sources? _____

_____

_____

Helpful call numbers: _____

_____   _____

Subjects/keywords: _____

_____   _____

Can you read and understand what you have found?

How will you keep track of your information?

Have you found enough information to answer your questions?

Figure 4.70 **Music and the Media Center**

Note: Music teacher designs question sheets in radial and nonlinear patterns of sections of questions. The linear form seen here largely diminishes the originality of their presentation, which is very appealing and motivating for students. Many of these questions require subtle critical thinking. They are part of the complex thinking required to find, read, and extract information from appropriate resources.

Library Question Sheet 1

Instructions:

Go to the library to find your answers.

Use computers, encyclopedias, and dictionaries.

If one question is difficult to find, skip it, then go back to it later.

    To begin, start anywhere!

Your name is: _____

Bartok's first name was: _____

Chopin was born in a city with a very strange name. What is it? _____

From which country does the bagpipe come? _____

Manuel de Falla wrote a ballet about a weird hat. How many corners did it have? _____

Gilbert and Sullivan became a very successful team for writing operettas.

    Who wrote the music? _____ And who wrote the lyrics (words)? _____

Does the zither have more or fewer than ten strings? _____

What style of music did Scott Joplin write? _____

What instrument did Albert Einstein play? _____

How old was Schubert when he died? _____

Was Mozart alive when Beethoven was born? _____

How many members in the group, "The Beatles?" _____

What was Duke Ellington's real first name? _____

Arrange the four following instruments in size, smallest to largest:
    cello, bass, violin, viola.

_____ _____ _____ _____

Figure 4.70 **(continued from page 147)**

Which of these composers was not born in Russia: Rachmaninov, Scriabin, or Holst? (Circle one.)

Who wrote more symphonies, Haydn or Brahms? (Circle one.)

Name four string instruments that you find in any orchestra.

_____ _____ _____ _____

Besides classical, name three other styles of music:

_____ _____ _____

Who wrote "The Mikado" (two names)? _____ _____

Which is faster, allegro or adagio? (Circle one.)

For what style of music is Bob Marley noted? _____

What word do these notes spell?

_____ _____ _____ _____

What instrument did Clara Schumann play? _____

Who lived longer, Bob Marley or Wolfgang Mozart? (Circle one.)

Figure 4.71 **Music and the Media Center**

Library Question Sheet 2

Instructions:
Go to the library to find your answers.
Use computers, encyclopedias, and dictionaries.
If one question is difficult to find, skip it, then go back to it later.
To begin, start anywhere!

Your name is: _____

How old was Benny Goodman when he began to play the clarinet? _____
   He was known as the King of ___ ___ ___ ___ ___.

Beethoven was born in the city of _____

Carlos Chavez was a famous composer from what country? _____

Duets have how many players? _____

"Enigma Variations" is a famous composition for orchestra written by Edward Elgar.

   What does "Enigma" mean? _____

A fandango is a lively dance from which country? _____

How many keys do modern pianos have? _____

Italy had many great composers.
   Who was born first, Monteverdi or Palestrina? (Circle one)

Name two instruments that Native Americans use in their music.

   _____   _____

Arrange the four following instruments in size, smallest to largest:
   English horn, bassoon, piccolo, oboe.

   _____   _____   _____   _____

   In what family of musical instruments are they? _____

Name a famous orchestra conductor. _____

Is Charles Ives still alive? _____

Figure 4.72 | **Music and the Media Center**

Music Room Question Sheet 1

Instructions:
Complete your work in the music room.
If one question is difficult to find, skip it, then go back to it later.
To begin, start anywhere!

My name is: _____

What are three string instruments you might find in a small jazz band?

_____   _____   _____

A Dixieland band uses a completely different string instrument than a small jazz band.
     What is it? _____

Does the Irish harp have a neck?_____ How many pedals does it have?_____

     What would happen to a harp player if he/she annoyed his/her listeners? _____
     When playing the harp, what is the word that means sliding the fingers rapidly across the
     strings? ___ ___ ___ ___ s ___ ___ ___ ___
     Listen to it. Does it sound high, low, or both? (Circle one.)

From which country does the kantele come? _____
     What three materials are used to make its strings?

_____   _____   _____

     How many sound holes does it have? _____

What is used to pluck the strings in a spinet? _____

Who invented or "introduced" the first electric guitar?_____

Where is the krar from? ___ ___ ___ ___ o ___ ___ ___ How many strings does it have? _____

Go to the Yueqin.
     What sound does the "e" have? _____ What sound does the "q" have?_____

Does the koto have a sound hole?_____ How many strings does a koto usually have?_____

What helps to amplify the sound on a vina? (These make it sound louder.) _____

Do you use a bow when you play the Rebab Andaluz? _____

     From which country does it come? _____ How many tuning pegs does it have?_____

Figure 4.73   **Music and the Media Center**

Music Room Question Sheet 2

Instructions:
Complete your work in the music room.
If one question is difficult to find, skip it, then go back to it later.
To begin, start anywhere!

My name is: _____ _____

Name a string instrument of Southeast Asia. _ _ _ _ _ - _ _ _ _

    Does it sound higher or lower than a cello? _____

In chamber groups, how many instruments are there in the piano trio? _____

    Name the string instruments in this group. _____

How many instruments in a wind octet? _____

    Name the string instruments in a wind octet. _____

What covers the beaters for a cimbalom? _____
    Listen to the cimbalom. Does it sound high, low, or both? (Circle one.)
    When pronouncing the word "cimbalom," does the "c" have an "s" or "k" sound? _____

    What is the name of the pedal? _____

From what are the strings on a classical guitar made? __ __ __ __ __
    Is the sound of a classical guitar bright & loud or mellow & soft or both? (Circle one.)

Listen to the Les Paul electric guitar. How many powerful pick-ups does it have? _____

    After whom is this guitar named? _____

If you were making a scary movie, which instrument would be best: kamanche, sarangi, or erhu? (Circle one.)

Who was the first Hawaiian to slide something along the strings of a pedal steel guitar?
__ __ __ __ __ __   __ __ __ __ __ __
    How many necks does the pedal steel guitar have? _____

Which sounds lower, a soprano saxophone or a viola? (Circle one.)

There is an ancient Chinese instrument called the pipa. What does the word "pipa" mean? _____

Figure 4.74 **Music and the Media Center**

Samples

Library Question Sheet 1

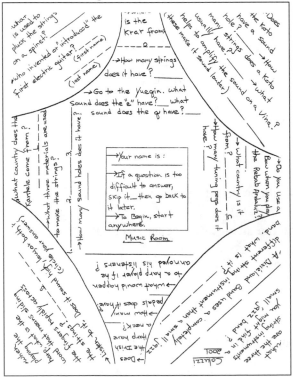

Library Question Sheet 2

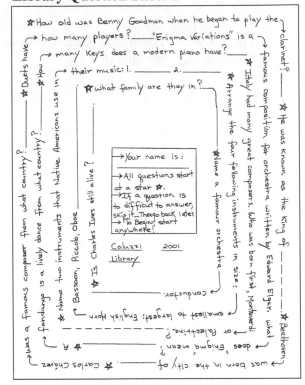

Music Room Question Sheet 1

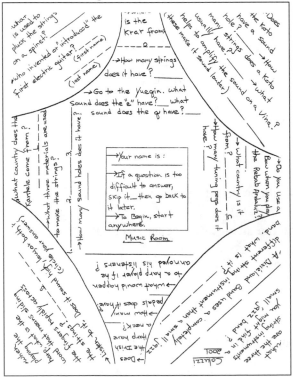

Music Room Question Sheet 2

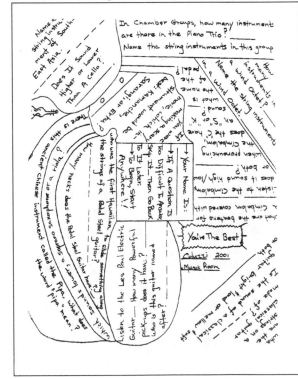

Figure 4.75   **Music and the Media Center**

Assessment Checklist

Name————————————————————

Evaluator————————————————————

Note: Checklist is based on level of independence in conducting research.

	Basic	**Proficient**	**Exemplary**
Understands the research task			
Determines appropriate resources for location of information			
Locates and accesses information			
Reads and understands information located			
Utilizes information to answer questions			
Self-evaluates and adjusts accordingly			

PQI (Personal Quest for Information)
Linda D. Sherouse, Library Media Generalist
Sherry Hoffman, Brenda Tharp, and Wendy Crowley, Grade 6 Teachers
North Hampton School (PreK-8)
201 Atlantic Ave., North Hampton, NH 03862
603-964-5501
lsherouse@sau2.k12.nh.us

Grade Level: Grade 6

Unit Overview: PQI is a personalized research unit that capitalizes on students' natural curiosity. It is designed to teach students how to find the information they seek, utilize it in an ethical and effective manner, and present it in a self-selected form. PQI is one step in a PreK through eighth grade information skills progression leading toward a culminating oratorical speech in the final years. Students suggest three topics of personal interest. The library media generalist and teachers then determine those topics best suited for each student with attention to abilities and special needs, information accessibility, and audience. Then the process of their Personal Quest for Information begins.

Time Frame: 20–22 school days

Content Area Standards: North Hampton School Standards and Benchmarks, North Hampton, New Hampshire

Language Arts—Grade 6 Standards:
Standard 4. Students will read, interpret, and respond to a variety of literary and informational texts, making connections to personal experiences, to other texts and to the world.
4.1 Use personal criteria (e.g. personal interest and skill, knowledge of authors and genres, text difficulty, recommendation of others) to select, read and enjoy reading material.
4.2 Apply reading skills and strategies to a variety of familiar literary passages and informational texts.
4.3 Read a variety of fiction and non-fiction texts.
4.4 Use strategies to respond to literary and informational texts (e.g. advance judgements with references to text, other works, other authors, non print media, and personal knowledge).
4.6 Understand main ideas, themes, purposes, and point of view (e.g. first and third person) of literary and information texts.
4.8 Understand that a single text can elicit a variety of responses and interpretations.
4.9 Make inferences based on explicit and implicit information in texts.

Standard 5. Students will use a variety of print and non-print resources to locate and gather information.
5.1 Use a variety of sources for research topics (e.g. electronic media).
5.2 Select and use a variety of resources to gather information.
5.3 Evaluate, compare, combine and contrast information from a variety of sources.
5.4 Present information in a variety of print and non-print forms.

Information Power Information Literacy Standards and Indicators: 1.1, 1.2, 1.3, 1.4, 1.5, 2.2, 2.3, 2.4, 3.1, 3.2, 3.3, 3.4, 4.1, 4.2, 5.1, 5.2, 5.3, 6.1, 6.2, 8.2, 8.3

Cooperative Teaching Plan:

Library Media Generalist Will:

- Update pathfinder checklist based on new resources available. Prior to the start of the unit, schedule lab time for students to review subscription online sources:
  - Curriculum Resource by NewsBank
  - KidsPage by NewsBank
  - Infotrac SuperTom Jr.
  - Grolier Online
  - WilsonWeb
- Teach a lesson using the overhead in the library to look at the Pathfinder as a group and differentiate between sources and tools (e.g., The Internet is a tool—not a source. Grolier Online is a tool for accessing the *New Book of Knowledge*, which is an encyclopedia source. Curriculum Resource and Infotrac are tools for accessing newspaper or magazine articles from a variety of sources).
- Teach a lesson in which students examine overheads of a wide variety of Internet pages and learn how to validate them by reading and interpreting URLs.
- Teach students the five Ws and one H of cyberspace as found on <www.media-awareness.ca/eng/webaware/tipsheets/w5.htm>.
- Teach students the differences between book publication and Internet dissemination of information.
- Lead a discussion of plagiarism and ownership of information.
- Present the interview as a resource and examine the varying expertise of those adults with whom students have daily contact.
- Provide one-on-one assistance with topic definition and initial direction for research, as requested by the teacher.
- Assist students during research phase of the project.

Teachers Will:

- Introduce students to the "PQI Challenge."
- Teach double-column note taking skills in which students differentiate between the main idea and its supporting details in articles of varying length, ordered by difficulty.
- Provide all process checklists and documentation.
- Check individual progress at checkpoints.
- Provide students with a calendar of the expected timetable for the unit.
- Provide students with rubrics and quality standards.
- Provide assistance to students or seek assistance of the LMG when inadequate information has been found.
- Instruct students in the construction of a bibliography.

Resources:

Print

Academic American. Danbury, Connecticut: Grolier, 2001.

Encyclopedia Americana. Danbury, Connecticut: Grolier, 2001.

Garraty, John A., ed. *American Heritage 35 Year Chronological Subject Guide.* New York: American Heritage Press, 1990.

National Geographic Index, 1888–1988. Washington, DC: National Geographic Society, 1989.

National Geographic Index, 1989–1998. Washington, DC: National Geographic Society, 1999.

National Geographic Index, 1999. Washington, DC: National Geographic Society, 2000.

National Geographic Index, 2000. Washington, DC: National Geographic Society, 2001.

New Book of Knowledge. Danbury, Connecticut: Grolier, 2001.

World Book Encyclopedia. Chicago: World Book, Inc., 2001.

Electronic

"Knowing What's What and What's Not: The Five W's (and One "H") of Cyberspace." *Media Awareness Network.* 11 July 2001.
<www.media-awareness.ca/eng/webaware/tipsheets/w5.htm>.

Online Databases (subscription required):
Grolier Online
InfoTrac
NewsBank
Wilson Web

Community Members

A wide range of community members with an interest in or knowledge of topics under study.

Product or Culminating Activity: Students are allowed to choose from a varied list of possible presentation formats (video, enactment, new interview, map, model, mural, illustration, report, musical or dance presentation, skit) based on Howard Gardner's theory of multiple intelligences in addition to a written presentation submitted for final teacher review.

Assessment Overview: Assessment is an ongoing part of the process. Each of the five sections of the PQI project has its own rubric for evaluation, with a total of 100 points possible for the project as a whole.

Figure 4.76   **PQI (Personal Quest for Information)**

Challenge

This challenge is made up of five sections, each with a special purpose. You will receive a separate page for each step with specific directions and expectations. The final grade will be based on the total points earned throughout the challenge.

The five sections and possible points for each are as follows:

1. MY QUESTIONS   **(10)**

This will include what you want to know about your topic at the start and what you hope to learn.

2. MY SEARCH PROCESS   **(10)**

This will be an overview of the steps, problems, and successes in your search for information.
It will also include:

    PATHFINDER CHECKLIST   **(5)**

    on which you will keep track of places you have searched.

    BIBLIOGRAPHY FORMS   **(5)**

    which you must fill out as you utilize each resource.

3. WHAT I HAVE LEARNED

    THE NOTES   **(10)**

    THE PRESENTATION   **(30)**

This is where you will share what you have learned with your class. YOU will select how you want to accomplish this.

4. WHAT THIS MEANS TO ME   **(15)**

This is where you will tell what you have learned about research and yourself as a researcher.

5. BIBLIOGRAPHY   **(15)**

This will be an accurate list of all materials used. You MUST use three different sources of information. Examples below:

newspaper	periodical (magazine)	personal interview
book	valid Internet sites	what else?

POSSIBLE TOTAL POINTS**   **(100)**

**All points will be based on QUALITY of work. Written work MUST be carefully edited and follow quality paper standards, which includes presentation in ink or typed.

Figure 4.77   **PQI (Personal Quest for Information)**

Pathfinder Checklist

Pathfinder Notes

Name_____

KEYWORDS:

I looked in the:
_____ Library Catalog (automated)

Library Resources:
(found in favorites folder on Internet)

NewsBank:
_____ Curriculum Resource
_____ SchoolMate KidsPage

InfoTrac:
_____ Periodicals
_____ Newspapers
_____ Reference Books
_____ Followed a "see" or "see also"
      cross reference

Grolier Online:
_____ Encyclopedia Americana
_____ Grolier Multimedia Encyclopedia
_____ New Book of Knowledge
_____ Book of Popular Science
_____ America the Beautiful

Wilson Web:
_____ put check in biographies box

Print Encyclopedia Indexes:
_____ World Book
_____ Encyclopedia Americana
_____ New Book of Knowledge
_____ Academic American

Other:
_____ Internet
_____ Other CD resources
      (LOOK in the CD-ROM Carousel)
_____ Other Reference books
_____ Possible interviews
_____ National Geographic Index
_____ American Heritage Index
_____ Checked with Librarian

Figure 4.78   **PQI (Personal Quest for Information)**

Project Points

Project	Part	My Score
#1	**My Questions** **(10 points)**	_____
#2	**My Search Process** **(10 points)**	
	Pathfinder Checklist (5 points)	_____
	Bibliography Forms (5 points)	_____
	My Search Process Questions (10 points)	_____
#3	**What I Have Learned** **(40 points)**	_____
	Notes (10 points)	_____
	The Presentation (30 points)	_____
#4	**What This Means to Me** **(15 points)**	_____
#5	**Bibliography** **(15 points)**	_____
	MY TOTAL	_____

Figure 4.79   **PQI (Personal Quest for Information)**

Weekly Reflection Sheet

Complete the following and meet with your teacher or librarian.

How has your search been going for you this week?

_____

_____

_____

_____

_____

_____

_____

How can a teacher or librarian help you?

_____

_____

_____

_____

_____

_____

_____

Teacher/Librarian Initials:

_____

Figure 4.80   PQI (Personal Quest for Information)

#1 My Questions (10 points)

My PQI topic is _____

Some things I already know are:

Some questions I would like to answer about my topic are:

I selected this topic because:

Figure 4.81   PQI (Personal Quest for Information)

My Questions

10 Point Rubric

Quality	Possible Points	Score
1. Things I know (three or more facts)	3	_____
2. Questions (4 or more questions)	3	_____
3. Reason topic selected (explains your interest)	2	_____
4. Follows quality paper standards	2	_____
TOTAL		_____

Figure 4.82 | **PQI (Personal Quest for Information)**

#2 My Search Process (20 points)

(5) Pathfinder checklist   (5) Bibliography forms   (10) Search Process questions

A. Pathfinder checklist:
Check off each resource that you explored for information.

B. Bibliography forms:
Fill out a bibliography form for each source you will use for any notes. You must use three different sources. (Hint: Staple a form to any articles you have printed or to any notes that you have taken.)

C. My Search Process:
Answer each question below carefully and completely.

1. What steps did you take to find information? (What did you do first, second...?)

2. What problems did you have in finding information and how did you solve them?

3. What were your best sources of information?

4. How did other people (friends, teachers, parents) help you? Be specific.

Figure 4.83 | **PQI (Personal Quest for Information)**

My Search Process

10 Point Rubric

Quality	Possible Points	Score
1. Pathfinder checklist shows good effort.	5	_____
2. I showed the teacher completed bibliography forms from three different sources.	5	_____
3. MY SEARCH PROCESS questions follow quality paper standards (edited and written in complete sentences).	2	_____
4. Each question is answered with specific information.	2 (each question)	_____
	TOTAL	_____

Figure 4.84   PQI (Personal Quest for Information)

#3 What I Have Learned (40 points)

A. Notes (10):
   1. Notes must be passed in on the day of your presentation.
   2. All notes will be taken in two-column form.
   3. The number of notes should reflect two weeks' worth of research work.

B. The Presentation (30): YOU BECOME THE TEACHER!

Now it is time to share what you have learned. You must include the major findings or main ideas from your research. Share this in an interesting way to help your audience understand what you have learned. Presentation time must be 3 to 5 minutes.

   Consider your own style and consider your audience. Some possible ideas are:

   *Make a video.   *Become the person you researched.
   *Conduct a news interview.   *Create a map.
   *Construct a model   *Create a mural.
   *Illustrate your findings.   *Write a report (with cover & title page).
   *Share information with music or dance. *Write/perform a skit.

Figure 4.85   PQI (Personal Quest for Information)

Notes

10 Point Rubric

Quality	Possible Points	Score
1. Notes passed in on day of presentation.	2	_____
2. All notes are in two-column form.	2	_____
3. Number of notes equal to two weeks' worth of research and work.	6	_____
	TOTAL	_____

Figure 4.86   PQI (Personal Quest for Information)

The Presentation

30 Point Rubric

Quality	Possible Points	Score
Points will be earned based on your presentation rubrics. The 3 to 5 minute time limit must also be considered.	40	_____
	TOTAL	_____

Figure 4.87 PQI (Personal Quest for Information)

Presentation Rubric for a SHADOW BOX/DIORAMA

_____ neatly made
_____ sturdy construction
_____ eye appeal/colorful
_____ has to do with topic
_____ separate paragraph, carefully written & edited
_____ explanation with required information
_____ eye contact with audience
_____ voice loud and clear
_____ follows time limits
_____ completed when due
        *If shared as a group:
_____ all participated equally

Name _____

Comments _____
_____
_____
_____

Total Points _____   Grade _____

0=not at all   1=somewhat   2=satisfactory   3=excellent

Figure 4.88 PQI (Personal Quest for Information)

Presentation Rubric for a MODEL

_____ looks like what it represents
_____ big enough to see details
_____ parts clearly labeled
_____ sturdy/tough construction
_____ neatly done
_____ has to do with topic
_____ separate paragraph, carefully written & edited
_____ explanation with required information
_____ eye contact with audience
_____ voice loud and clear
_____ follows time limits
_____ completed when due
        *If shared as a group:
_____ all participated equally

Name _____

Comments _____
_____
_____
_____

Total Points _____   Grade _____

0=not at all   1=somewhat   2=satisfactory   3=excellent

Figure 4.89 PQI (Personal Quest for Information)

Presentation Rubric for a VIDEO

_____ interesting to audience
_____ loud, clear voices
_____ appropriately done (rated G!)
_____ includes required information
_____ knew lines and stayed in role
_____ good use of costume and props
_____ good background & lighting
_____ camera held steady, not jumpy
_____ follows time limits
_____ completed when due
        *If shared as a group:
_____ all participated equally

Name _____

Comments _____
_____
_____
_____

Total Points _____   Grade _____

0=not at all   1=somewhat   2=satisfactory   3=excellent

| Figure 4.90 | PQI (Personal Quest for Information) |

Presentation Rubric for a WRITTEN PIECE

_____ neatly done/quality paper standards
_____ carefully edited
_____ ink or typed
_____ eye catching cover with title, author & visual
_____ includes required information
_____ stays on topic
_____ flows well
_____ follows the RECIPE!
_____ completed when due

Name _____

Comments _____

_____

_____

_____

Total Points _____   Grade _____

0=not at all   1=somewhat   2=satisfactory   3=excellent

| Figure 4.91 | PQI (Personal Quest for Information) |

Presentation Rubric for a SONG/INTERPRETIVE DANCE

_____ words (actions) clearly understood
_____ includes required information
_____ words (actions) clearly connected to topic
_____ makes sense
_____ good tempo for material presented
_____ holds audience attention
_____ knew lines (dance)
_____ long enough to present all information
_____ completed when due
*If shared as a group:
_____ all participated equally

Name _____

Comments _____

_____

_____

_____

Total Points _____   Grade _____

0=not at all   1=somewhat   2=satisfactory   3=excellent

| Figure 4.92 | PQI (Personal Quest for Information) |

Presentation Rubric for a GAME

_____ neatly done
_____ creative/eye appeal
_____ directions clearly stated on separate paper, in ink or typed
_____ directions carefully edited
_____ includes required information
_____ sticks to topic being taught/shared
_____ makes sense/works!
_____ fun & informative for the audience
_____ whole class participates
_____ not too hard but challenging
_____ follows time limits
_____ completed when due
*If shared as a group:
_____ all participated equally

Name _____

Comments _____

_____

_____

_____

Total Points _____   Grade _____

0=not at all   1=somewhat   2=satisfactory   3=excellent

Figure 4.93 **PQI (Personal Quest for Information)**

Presentation Rubric for an ORAL PIECE

_____ voice is loud and clear (no monotone)
_____ makes eye contact with audience
_____ interesting to audience
_____ familiar with text (can pronounce all words)
_____ includes all required information
_____ includes a quality visual connected to topic
_____ specific and on topic
_____ follows time limits
_____ completed when due

Name _____

Comments _____

_____

_____

_____

Total Points _____ Grade _____

Figure 4.94 **PQI (Personal Quest for Information)**

Presentation Rubric for a SKIT

_____ creative/interesting to audience
_____ face audience/speak clearly
_____ includes costumes and props
_____ players know parts well
_____ required information included
_____ sticks to topic (appropriate)
_____ clearly well planned
_____ follows time limits
_____ completed when due
*If shared as a group:
_____ all participated equally

Name _____

Comments _____

_____

_____

_____

Total Points _____ Grade _____

Figure 4.95 **PQI (Personal Quest for Information)**

Presentation Rubric for a POSTER/MURAL

_____ neatly done
_____ has eye appeal/creatively organized
_____ clearly shows what you are trying to teach/share
_____ labeled/quality paper standards
_____ letters/pictures large enough to be seen
_____ explanation with required information
_____ eye contact with audience
_____ voice loud and clear
_____ follows time limits
_____ completed when due
*If shared as a group:
_____ all participated equally

Name _____

Comments _____

_____

_____

_____

Total Points _____ Grade _____

0=not at all   1=somewhat   2=satisfactory   3=excellent

Figure 4.96   **PQI (Personal Quest for Information)**

Presentation Rubric for OVERHEADS/SLIDES

_____ neatly done
_____ clear writing/carefully edited
_____ creatively designed with eye appeal
_____ color used if possible
_____ includes required information
_____ clear explanation given
_____ holds audience interest
_____ eye contact with audience
_____ voice loud and clear
_____ follows time limits
_____ completed when due
    *If shared as a group:
_____ all participated equally

Name _____

Comments _____

_____

_____

_____

Total Points _____   Grade _____

0=not at all   1=somewhat   2=satisfactory   3=excellent

Figure 4.97   **PQI (Personal Quest for Information)**

Presentation Rubric for a PUPPET SHOW

_____ puppets match what you are sharing/teaching
_____ puppets have eye appeal
_____ puppets are visible to all
_____ puppeteers out of sight
_____ knows lines well
_____ voices can be heard clearly (good expression)
_____ sticks to topic
_____ includes required information
_____ creative/entertaining for audience
_____ follows time limits
_____ completed when due
    *If shared as a group:
_____ all participated equally

Name _____

Comments _____

_____

_____

_____

Total Points _____   Grade _____
0=not at all   1=somewhat   2=satisfactory   3=excellent

Figure 4.98 PQI (Personal Quest for Information)

#4 What This Means to Me (15 points)

Answer the following questions about this project and yourself as a researcher. Be specific!

What was easiest for you in this whole process?

_____

_____

What did you find most difficult?

_____

_____

What will you do differently the next time you do research?

_____

_____

What things would make you "pat yourself on the back"?

_____

_____

What advice do you have for teachers in guiding students with research?

_____

_____

_____

Figure 4.99 PQI (Personal Quest for Information)

What This Means to Me

15 Point Rubric

Quality	Possible Points	Score
1. Follows quality paper standards (includes editing, paragraphs, complete sentences).	5	_____
2. Each answer includes specific information or reasons.	2 each	_____
	TOTAL	_____

Figure 4.100   **PQI (Personal Quest for Information)**

#5 The Bibliography (15 points)

1. You must list all references used in your project.

2. Each bibliography entry must follow correct format. (Follow sample guide sheet carefully.)

3. Entries must be listed in alphabetical order by the author's last name. If the author is not given, use the first MAIN word in the title.

4. Bibliography must be passed in on the day of your presentation.

Figure 4.101   **PQI (Personal Quest for Information)**

The Bibliography

15 Point Rubric

Quality	Possible Points	Score
1. Follows quality paper standards	5	_____
2. Follows correct bibliography format	5	_____
3. Entries listed in alphabetical order by author's last name	5	_____
	TOTAL	_____

Question Yourself: Discover Your Human Body

Kim Grimes, Teacher-Librarian
Karla Ahumada, Grade 3 ESL and Tom Dodd, Grade 3 Gifted and Talented
Corbett Elementary School
5949 E. 29th Street, Tucson, AZ 95711
520-584-4900
kim.grimes@tusd.k12.az.us

Grade Level: 3 ESL and 3 Gifted and Talented

Unit Overview: Question Yourself: Discover Your Human Body focuses on a third grade science curriculum unit, uses the FOSS (Full Option Science System) kit entitled *Human Body* in the classroom, and employs inquiry based research in the library. The goal is student brainstorming of questions and subsequent location of answers to their inquiries. As a result of this unit, students will: 1) formulate questions on the human body; 2) view and navigate Web sites on body systems in order to locate information; 3) choose one system to study and answer three questions about it; 4) use a variety of print and nonprint resources to locate information; 5) write a five paragraph essay based on their research.

Time Frame: 4 to 5 weeks on a flexible schedule

Content Area Standards: Tucson Unified School District CORE Curriculum for the 21st Century
<http://instech.tusd.k12.az.us/CORE/corefoun.htm>

Language Arts, Grade 3
Standard R-F3. Reading: Use reading comprehension strategies such as drawing conclusions, summarizing, making predictions, identifying cause and effect and differentiating between fiction and nonfiction.
PO 4. identify cause-and-effect relationships.

Standard W-F1. Writing: Use the writing process, including generating topics, participating in prewriting activities, drafting, revising ideas and editing to complete effectively a variety of writing tasks.
PO 1. generate topics through prewriting activities (e.g., brainstorming, webbing, mapping, drawing, writer's notebook, K-W-L charts, scaffolds, group discussion);
PO 3. write a first draft with the necessary components for a specific genre;
PO 4. revise draft content (e.g., organization, relevant details, clarity);
PO 5. edit revised draft using resources (e.g., dictionary, word lists and banks, thesaurus, spell checker, glossary, style manual, grammar and usage reference);
PO 6. proofread revised draft;
PO 7. present final copy according to purpose (e.g., read aloud, display, publish, mail, send, perform).

Note: The Northwest Regional Educational Laboratory's Six Traits of Writing <http://www.nwrel.org/eval/writing/> are utilized at the state and local level. This unit focuses on "Organization," "Ideas and Content," and "Word Choice."

Standard (unnumbered). Listening and Speaking: Give and follow multiple step directions. Prepare and deliver information by generating topics, identifying the audience, and organizing ideas, facts, or opinions for presenting a report.
Standard (unnumbered). Listening and Speaking: Prepare and deliver information by generating topics; identifying the audience; and organizing ideas, facts or opinions for a variety of speaking purposes such as giving directions, relating personal experiences, telling a story or presenting a report.

Science, Grade 3

Standard SC4-F3. Life Science: Identify the basic structures and functions of plants and animals.
PO 1. identify basic animal structures;
PO 2. describe the functions of basic animal structures.

Standard SC4-F5. Life Science: Recognize that component parts make up the human body systems (e.g., digestive, muscular, skeletal).
PO 1. identify major organs within systems (i.e., musculo-skeletal system).

Note: Use FOSS Kit *Human Body* and inquiry based learning to achieve the following Goals.

FOSS Human Body Kit Goals, Grades 3–4
The Human Body module consists of four sequential investigations that engage students in thoughtful activities about the form and function of a most remarkable machine, their own body. FOSS expects students to:
- Observe and investigate the human skeletal and muscle systems.
- Gain experience with use of photographs, diagrams, and model bones to gather information.
- Acquire vocabulary associated with human skeletal and muscle systems.
- Use scientific thinking processes to conduct investigations and build explanations: observing, communicating, comparing, and organizing.

Information Power Information Literacy Standards and Indicators: 1.1, 1.3, 1.4, 1.5, 2.1, 2.2, 2.3, 2.4, 3.1, 3.2, 3.3, 3.4, 4.1, 5.2, 6.1, 7.1, 7.2, 8.2, 8.3, 9.1, 9.2, 9.3

Cooperative Teaching Plan:

Library Media Specialist Will:
- Work with the classroom teacher to create learning centers in the classroom.
- Develop and photocopy graphic organizers ("Question" sheet, Note taking sheet)
- Locate appropriate Web sites and place on school home page.
- Review simple vs. complex questions (whole class).
- Using a Proxima projector, show students how to navigate the school's Web site to locate pre-selected Web sites on the human body (whole class).
- Explain responsible use of technology and explain how to navigate Web sites (whole class).

- Supervise students in brainstorming complex questions and writing them down on their Question Sheets while viewing Web sites (whole class).
- Direct students in cutting up questions, identifying the system to which they belong, and taping them onto big sheets of paper labeled by system (whole class).
- Teach students how to use an index, table of contents, and multimedia—CD-ROMs, Internet, etc. (system group).
- Teach students to take notes, identify bibliographic information, and record them (system group).
- Visit classroom and focus on "Organization," "Ideas and Content," and "Word Choice" in the 6+1 Traits™ of Writing system < http://www.nwrel.org/EVAL/WRITING/>.
- Show students how to cut up notes and put them in order under a topic sentence.
- Demonstrate how to write an introductory and concluding paragraph.
- Demonstrate the responsible use of the Alphasmart laptop computer.
- Review rough drafts.
- Grade research process.
- Help teachers to grade essays using 6+1 Traits™ rubrics.

Teachers Will:
- Work with the teacher-librarian to create learning centers in the classroom.
- Introduce simple vs. complex questions.
- Introduce FOSS Kit *Human Body* and teach kit in the classroom.
- Review questions that are labeled by system on big sheets of paper.
- Divide students into five system groups according to their interest in a particular system or series of questions on a system.
- Supervise in-class completion of rough drafts and typing of final drafts on Alphasmart laptop computers.
- Grade essays using 6+1 Traits™ rubrics.
- Provide opportunity for students to share their essays and knowledge.

Resources:

Print
Cromwell, Sharon. *Bodywise* Series. Westport, Connecticut: Heinemann, 1998.

Parker, Steve. *Look At Your Body* Series *(Blood, Skeleton, Digestion, Lungs, Senses)*. Brookfield, Connecticut: Copper Beach, 1996, 1997.

Stille, Darlene. *A True Book* Series *(Digestive System, Nervous System, Respiratory System, Circulatory System)*. New York: Children's Press, 1997.

World Book Student Discovery Encyclopedia. Chicago: World Book, Inc., 2000.

Electronic
McGann, Andrew. *A Look Inside the Human Body*. 9 July 2001.
    <http://bart.northnet.com.au/~amcgann/body/

Microsoft Encarta 1998. CD-ROM. Redmond, Washington: Microsoft Corporation, 1998.

Oliver, Brooke, et al. "Look into the Human Body." *ThinkQuest Library*. 3 February 2002
    <http://library.thinkquest.org/J0112964/>.

"The Virtual Body." *Medtropolis*. 9 July 2001 <http://medtropolis.com/vbody.asp>.

Equipment
FOSS (Full Option Science Systems) Human Body module <www.fossweb.com>
Proxima projector connected to a Compaq computer

Product or Culminating Activity: Students will synthesize all of the information garnered during the research project and apply it to the writing of a formal five paragraph essay.

Assessment Overview: Grade on research activity is either Pass or Fail based on the quality of notes and the variety of sources used (a minimum of two is required). Five paragraph essay is graded using the 6+1 Traits™ of Writing rubrics <http://www.nwrel.org/EVAL/WRITING/>.

Extension/Adaptation: Rather than writing a formal research essay, consider making a pop-up book or creating an interactive body museum.

Figure 4.102   **Question Yourself: Discover Your Human Body**

Question Sheet

NAME:————————————————————————

TOPIC:———————————————————————

QUESTION: ——————————————————————
————————————————————————————————

QUESTION: ——————————————————————
————————————————————————————————

QUESTION: ——————————————————————
————————————————————————————————

QUESTION: ——————————————————————
————————————————————————————————

QUESTION: ——————————————————————
————————————————————————————————

QUESTION: ——————————————————————
————————————————————————————————

QUESTION: ——————————————————————
————————————————————————————————

Figure 4.103   **Question Yourself: Discover Your Human Body**

Note Taking Sheet

NAME:————————————————————

TOPIC:————————————————————

QUESTION: ——————————————————— ?

REF# ____ Page# ____	REF# ____ Page# ____
REF# ____ Page# ____	REF# ____ Page# ____
REF# ____ Page# ____	REF# ____ Page# ____

Figure 4.104	Question Yourself: Discover Your Human Body

Research Project Guidelines

NAME: _____

TOPIC: _____

Overview: You will be completing a research project for science. Your rough and final draft will be competed during writing time. Your Note Taking Sheets and final draft will be graded. Your rough copy will be edited by your classroom teacher or teacher-librarian. The final draft of the report must be typed. You will be able to type the final copy in class or in the library using an Alphasmart laptop computer.

Your rough draft and final paper will consist of the following parts:

1. **Cover page** that includes the title of your paper, your name, and the date. You will be shown an example of this page.
2. **Introductory paragraph,** which must include a topic sentence that identifies your topic. It may also include some background information that will help the reader understand the paper.
3. **The body** of your paper will include three paragraphs. Each paragraph will identify one of the three questions you researched. Each paragraph will contain a topic sentence, supporting details, and a strong concluding sentence. Transition words will be used also.
4. A **concluding paragraph** will complete your paper.
5. A **bibliography** will follow your written report. You will use a bibliography sheet while doing research to write down the author, title, publisher, and copyright date of the sources you used.

Notes and Note Taking Sheets DUE: _____

You will take notes on Note Making Sheets supplied by the library. You will be given three sheets. On the first sheet you will write your first question. On the second sheet, you will write your second question. On the third sheet you will write your third question.

As you find information that answers your questions, write down the source on a bibliography sheet. Number each bibliography entry and enter this Reference # on your Note Taking Sheet. Also include the author, title, publisher, and copyright date. Then use the Note Taking Sheet that has the question you are answering written on it. Read the information and put it in your own words using phrases and key words. Notes should contain no sentences.

Your note cards will be evaluated on a pass/fail scale.

Rough Draft DUE:

You will use your Note Taking Sheets to write the rough draft of your paper.

1. Read over all of your notes.
2. On a separate sheet paper, write an introductory paragraph. Include a topic sentence that introduces your topic. This paragraph can be personal and should "hook" the reader so s/he wants to read more.

Figure 4.104   **(continued from page 177)**

3. On a separate sheet of paper, write a paragraph that answers one of your questions. Make sure to include an effective topic sentence, supporting details, and a concluding sentence.
4. Repeat step 3 for each of your questions.
5. On a separate sheet of paper, write a concluding paragraph.
6. Beginning with your introductory paragraph and ending with your conclusion, arrange your sheets in the order you think makes the most sense for your audience. Number the pages. These sheets will be handed in.
7. Think about transition words and how to make your paragraphs flow together.
8. Write a rough draft in which you combine all of the paragraphs into one paper.

Bibliography: Follow the instructions you are given for creating your bibliography. It must be on a separate sheet of paper and handed in with your rough draft.

The rough draft and bibliography will be evaluated using the 6+1 Traits™ of Writing rubrics <http://www.nwrel.org/EVAL/WRITING/>.

Final Copy DUE: _____

After conferencing and revising your rough draft, you are ready to do the final copy of your research paper. You will type it at school.

It will be scored using the 6+1 Traits™ of Writing rubrics <http://www.nwrel.org/EVAL/WRITING/>.

'The Spirit of Do-right': Exploring the Lives of Famous African Americans

Jenny Foight-Cressman, Teacher-Librarian

Deena Hausman and Jane Drebes, Grade 5 Teachers

Stackpole Elementary School

1350 Strathmann Drive, Southampton, PA 18966

215-364-5980, ext. 1501

foigje@centennialsd.org

Grade Level: 5

Unit Overview: 'The Spirit of Do-right': Exploring the Lives of Famous African Americans draws its title from San Souci's *The Talking Eggs* in which an elder African-American woman praises a young girl for her generosity of soul. This inquiry based research unit explores the complex lives and unique contributions of African Americans while integrating the research process with an examination of slavery and resistance movements in this country. It seeks to extend knowledge of the African-American experience beyond the confines of "Black History Month" while teaching the research and report writing process, including brainstorming, topic selection, questioning, outlining, print and electronic researching, note taking, composing and editing, and recognizing intellectual property by constructing a bibliography of sources.

Time Frame: 20 hours of instruction in the library. Additional time, as needed, in the classroom and as homework

Content Area Standards: Pennsylvania Academic Standards
<http://www.pde.psu.edu/regs/chapter4.html>

Reading, Writing, Speaking and Listening

1.1 Learning to Read Independently
Standard G. Demonstrate after reading understanding and interpretation of both fiction and non-fiction text.
Indicator. Summarize the major ideas, themes or procedures of the text.
Indicator. Relate new information or ideas from the text to that learned through additional reading and media (e.g., film, audiotape).
Indicator. Clarify ideas and understandings through rereading and discussion.
Indicator. Make responsible assertions about the ideas from the text by citing evidence.
Indicator. Extend ideas found in the text.

1.2 Reading Critically in All Content Areas
Standard A. Read and understand essential content of informational texts and documents in all academic areas.
Indicator. Differentiate fact from opinion across texts.

Indicator. Distinguish between essential and nonessential information across a variety of texts, identifying stereotypes and exaggeration where present.

Indicator. Make inferences about similar concepts in multiple texts and draw conclusions.

Indicator. Evaluate text organization and content to determine the author's purpose and effectiveness.

Standard B. Use and understand a variety of media and evaluate the quality of material produced.

Indicator. Use a variety of media (e.g., computerized card catalogues, encyclopedias) for research.

Indicator. Evaluate the role of media as a source of both entertainment and information.

Standard C. Produce work in at least one literary genre that follows the conventions of the genre.

1.4 Types of Writing

Standard A. Write multi-paragraph informational pieces (e.g., essays, descriptions, letters, reports, instructions).

Indicator. Include cause and effect.

Indicator. Develop a problem and solution when appropriate to the topic.

Indicator. Use relevant graphics (e.g., maps, charts, graphs, tables, illustrations, photographs).

1.5 Quality of Writing

Standard A. Write with a sharp, distinct focus identifying topic, task and audience.

Standard B. Write using well-developed content appropriate for the topic.

Indicator. Gather, organize and select the most effective information appropriate for the topic, task and audience.

Indicator. Write paragraphs that have a topic sentence and supporting details.

Standard C. Write with controlled and/or subtle organization.

Indicator. Sustain a logical order within sentences and between paragraphs using meaningful transitions.

Indicator. Include an identifiable introduction, body and conclusion.

Standard D. Write with an understanding of the stylistic aspects of composition.

Indicator. Use different types and lengths of sentences.

Indicator. Use precise language including adjectives, adverbs, action verbs and specific details that convey the writer's meaning.

Indicator. Develop and maintain a consistent voice.

Standard E. Revise writing to improve organization and word choice; check the logic, order of ideas and precision of vocabulary.

Standard F. Edit writing using the conventions of language.

Indicator. Spell common, frequently used words correctly.

Indicator. Use capital letters correctly.

Indicator. Punctuate correctly (periods, exclamation points, question marks, commas, quotation marks, apostrophes).

Indicator. Use nouns, pronouns, verbs, adjectives, adverbs, conjunctions, prepositions and interjections properly.

Indicator. Use complete sentences (simple, compound, declarative, interrogative, exclamatory and imperative).

Indicator. Present and/or defend written work for publication when appropriate.

1.6 Speaking and Listening
Standard C. Participate in small and large group discussions and presentations.
Indicator. Present an oral reading.
Indicator. Deliver research reports.
Standard D. Use media for learning purposes.
Indicator. Access information on Internet.
Indicator. Discuss the reliability of information received on Internet sources.

1.8 Research
Standard A. Select and refine a topic for research.
Standard B. Locate information using appropriate sources and strategies.
Indicator. Evaluate the usefulness and qualities of the sources.
Indicator. Select appropriate sources (e.g., dictionaries, encyclopedias, other reference materials, interviews, observations, computer databases).
Indicator. Use tables of contents, indices, key words, cross-references and appendices.
Indicator. Use traditional and electronic search tools.
Standard C. Organize and present the main ideas from research.
Indicator. Take notes from sources using a structured format.
Indicator. Present the topic using relevant information.
Indicator. Credit sources using a structured format (e.g., author, title).

Proposed Academic Standards for History <http://www.pde.psu.edu/standard/histwhole.pdf>

History
8.2.6 Pennsylvania History, Grade 6
Standard D. Explain conflict and cooperation impacting Pennsylvania History
Indicator. Racial and ethnic relations.

8.3.6 United States History, Grade 6
Standard D. Explain conflict and cooperation impacting the United States.
Indicator. Racial and ethnic relations

Information Power Information Literacy Standards and Indicators: The research and report writing process meets all nine Information Power Information Literacy Standards and Indicators.

Cooperative Teaching Plan:

Teacher Librarian Will:
- Introduce the research project by reading *Wilma Unlimited* by Kathleen Krull.
- Discuss autobiography and biography as a genre.
- Model a method for extracting biographical information from a text and creating useful note cards.
- Review parts of a book including index, table of contents, and time lines.
- Assist students in searching for information in print and electronic sources (with teacher).
- Guide and conference individually with students during research process (with teacher).

- Monitor note taking (with Teacher).
- Discuss the concept of intellectual property/plagiarism.
- Demonstrate bibliographical citations.
- Conference with students over several drafts (with Teacher).
- Enjoy and celebrate student presentations of their writing.

Teachers Will:
- Introduce over thirty interesting people through short, captivating biographies.
- Encourage students to choose three people to investigate.
- Generate questions with students about what they would like to know about someone's life.
- Supervise students as they write questions on paper, manipulate them, and tape to form outline.
- Actively participate and contribute to lessons given by teacher-librarian in the library.
- Assist students in searching for information in print and electronic sources (with teacher-librarian).
- Guide and conference with students during research process (with teacher-librarian).
- Monitor note taking (with teacher-librarian).
- Model writing biographical report including mechanics and conventions.
- Conference with students over several drafts (with teacher-librarian).
- Assess student writing throughout project using rubrics.
- Enjoy and celebrate student presentations of their writing.

Resources:

Print
Krull, Kathleen. *Wilma Unlimited.* San Diego: Harcourt, 1996.
World Book Encyclopedia. Chicago: World Book, Inc., 2001.

A reserve collection of one hundred African-American reference sources, biographies, autobiographies, and historical fiction including:

Altman, Susan. *The Encyclopedia of African American Heritage.* New York: Facts on File, Inc., 1997.
Appiah, Kwame Anthony and Henry Louis Gates, eds. *Africana: The Encyclopedia of the African and African American Experience.* New York: Basic Civitas Books, 1999.
Hansen, Joyce. *Women of Hope: African Americans Who Made a Difference.* New York: Scholastic, 1998.
Kessler, James. *Distinguished African American Scientists of the Twentieth Century.* Phoenix: Oryx Press, 1996.
Knight, Judson. *African American Biography.* Detroit: UXL, 1998.
New York Public Library African American Desk Reference. New York: John Wiley & Sons, 1999.
Patrick, Diane. *The New York Public Library Amazing African American History: A Book of Answers for Kids.* New York: John Wiley & Sons, 1998.
Stewart, Jeffrey C. *1001 Things Everyone Should Know About African-American History.* New York: Doubleday, 1997.

Electronic

Britannica.com. 9 July 2001 <http://www.britannica.com/>
Microsoft Encarta Africana 2000. CD-ROM. Redmond, Washington: Microsoft Corporation, 2000.

Numerous Internet sites, depending on topic, including:

"The African American Journey." *World Book.* 3 February 2002
    <http://www2.worldbook.com/students/feature_index.asp>.
"African American Odyssey." *American Memory.* 18 Sept. 1998. 17 July 2001
    <http://memory.loc.gov/ammem/aaohtml/aohome.html>.
"The Faces of Science: African Americans in the Sciences." *Princeton University.* 9 Feb. 2001
    17 July 2001 <http://www.princeton.edu/~mcbrown/display/faces.html>.
"Heart and Soul: A Celebration of African American Music." *World Book.* 17 July 2001
    <http://www.worldbook.com/fun/aamusic/html/intro.htm>.
World Book Online. 9 July 2001 <http://www.worldbookonline.com/>. Requires subscription.

Product or Culminating Activity: Traditionally takes the form of a formal written report. The teaching team is currently discussing alternate formats such as *PowerPoint* presentations, Web pages, and project presentations.

Assessment Overview: Final student papers are assessed by a series of rubrics that look at both the process and product of the research/report writing experience. The Teacher-Librarian and the teacher meet regularly with the children throughout the process to help monitor progress and provide support and additional individual or small group instruction through mini-lessons when needed. While the Teacher-Librarian actively assists in the creation of the rubrics and participates in informal assessment or "kidwatching" throughout the assignment, the cooperating teacher completes the rubrics and assigns a final grade in language arts.

Research Project Guidelines

Name:_____

Topic:_____

Overview: You will be completing a research project for your Language Arts class. All of the research will be completed at school during Language Arts Block. Your rough draft will also be completed in school. Your teacher-librarian and your teacher will assist you in each step of this process. Your note cards and your rough copy will be graded. (This grade is called your "Working Research Grade.") Your rough copy will be revised in a conference with a teacher. Your final (good) copy of the report must be typed. You will be able to type the final copy at home after the revisions have been completed. The final copy will also receive a grade. All aspects of the research project will be part of the third marking period Writing grade.

Your rough draft and final paper will consist of the following parts:

1. **Cover page** that includes the title of your paper, your name, and the date. You will be shown an example of this page.
2. **Introductory paragraph** that identifies your topic and explains why you wanted to research it. It may also include some background information that will help the reader understand the paper.
3. **The body** of your paper will include five paragraphs. Each paragraph will discuss the answer to one
of your five questions. Each paragraph will have a topic sentence, supporting details, and a strong concluding sentence.
4. A **concluding paragraph** will complete your paper.
5. A **bibliography** will follow your written report. A bibliography is an alphabetical listing of all of the sources you used in writing your report. You will be given specific instructions on how to write the bibliography. **Be sure you write down the author, title, publisher, and date of publication of any sources you use.**

Notes and Note Taking Sheets DUE: _____

You will take notes on note cards supplied by the library. You will have six cards. On the first card you will write your first question. On the second card, you will write your second question. You will repeat this process for each of your questions. The sixth card is for miscellaneous information that you may want to include in your report.

As you find information that answers your questions, write down the source on a pink card. Include the author, title, date of publication, and the publisher. Then locate the note card that has the question written on it and jot down phrases and key words that will help you remember. Note cards should have no sentences.

Your note cards will be evaluated using the rubric.

Figure 4.105 **(continued from page 184)**

Rough Draft   DUE: _____
You will use your note cards to write the rough draft of your paper.

1. Read over all of your notes.
2. On a separate sheet of paper, write an introductory paragraph. Include your topic and why you chose it. If you think the reader will be unfamiliar with your subject, define what it is. This paragraph can be personal and should "hook" the reader so he/she wants to read more.
3. On another separate sheet of paper, write a paragraph that answers one of your questions. Make sure to include a good topic sentence, supporting details, and a concluding sentence.
4. Repeat step 3 for each of your questions.
5. On a separate sheet of paper, write a concluding paragraph.
6. Beginning with your introductory paragraph and ending with your conclusion, arrange your sheets in the order you think makes the most sense for your audience. Number the pages. **These sheets will be handed in.**
7. Think about transition words and how to make your paragraphs flow together.
8. Write a rough draft in which you combine all of the paragraphs into one paper.

Bibliography: Follow the instructions you are given for creating your bibliography. It must be on a separate sheet of paper and handed in with your rough draft.

The rough draft and bibliography will be evaluated using the rubric.

Final Copy DUE: _____
After conferencing and revising your rough draft, you are ready to do the final copy of your research paper. You may type it at home or in school. **It must be double spaced using a size 12 font. You must hand in two copies.**

It will be scored using the rubric.

Rough Draft and Bibliography Rubric

There are seven separate sheets representing seven paragraphs.	7 pts.	_____
Each body paragraph has a topic sentence.	5 pts.	_____
Each body paragraph has supporting details.	5 pts.	_____
Each body paragraph has a strong concluding sentence.	5 pts.	_____
The introductory paragraph hooks the reader.	2 pts.	_____
The concluding paragraph is strong and flows with the report.	2 pts.	_____
The rough draft is complete and uses strong transition words.	10 pts.	_____
The rough draft uses conventions and accurate spelling.	10 pts.	_____
The rough draft is neatly done.	5 pts.	_____
A bibliography is included.	1 pt.	_____
Alphabetical order	3 pts.	_____
Correct form	3 pts.	_____
Total		_____

Working Paper Score (average of notes and rough draft) _____

Notes Rubric

One question per card   10 pts.   _____

All questions answered   10 pts.   _____

Phrases and key words on cards   10 pts.   _____

At least three sources used   10 pts.   _____

Completed bibliography card for each source   10 pts.   _____

On-task behavior   10 pts.   _____

Organization of materials   10 pts.   _____

                                                               Total   _____

Final Copy of Research Paper Rubric

Physical Requirements:

Cover page with correct information   4 pts.   _____

Report including introduction, body, and conclusion   3 pts.   _____

Bibliography   1 pt.   _____

Two Copies   2 pts.   _____

Typed   1 pt.   _____

Appearance/Neatness   5 pts.   _____

Double Spaced   1 pt.   _____

Font Size 12 point   1 pt.   _____

Content—using the Pennsylvania Writing Assessment Holistic Scoring Guide on six levels of proficiency < http://www.pde.psu.edu/connections/currdevl/res4-b.htm>

Becca Stith, Library Media Specialist

Jo Dee McGraw, Cecilia Slenker, Lynette Pfingsten, and Whitney Rogers,

Grade 4 Teachers

Kathy Walzcuk, Computer Paraprofessional

Mission Trail Elementary School

13200 Mission Rd, Leawood, KS 66209

913-681-4375

bstith@bv229.k12.ks.us

Grade Level: 4

Unit Overview: State It! is an exciting project that allows students to acquire many information literacy skills. Students create a presentation board, brochure, float, and backpack which they present at Open House. The library media specialist, grade level teachers, and computer paraprofessional collaborate throughout the year on the extended project. Students learn to take notes on note cards (correct labeling), create bibliography cards, outlines, and graphs, using several sources of information. Graphs are created in computer class. Arrangement and coloring for the display board is presented in art class. Students locate and print state symbols and other visuals in the Library Media Center Instructional Technology lab.

Time Frame: Six to nine weeks, separated into four two-week sessions devoted to research on one of the four Roman Numerals of the outline. Each library media center meeting is 40 minutes. Projects are completed for Open House.

Content Area Standards: Blue Valley (Kansas) Schools Curriculum Standards

Social Studies Standards & Outcomes

History Standard: The student uses a working knowledge and understanding of significant individuals, groups, ideas, events, eras, and developments in the history of Kansas, the United States, and the world, utilizing essential analytical and research skills.

Benchmark 1: The student understands the significance of the contributions of important individuals and major developments in history.

Indicator 1. researches to determine the historical contributions of important local and regional individuals.

Indicator 4. compares and contrasts ways people communicate with each other now and long ago.

Indicator 5. describes the development and influence of tools on work and behavior.

Geography Standard: The student uses the working knowledge and understanding of the spatial organization of Earth's surface and relationship among people, places, and physical and human environments in order to explain the interactions that occur in our interconnected world.

Benchmark 2: Regions: The student analyzes the spatial organization of people, places, and environments that form regions on the Earth's surface.

Indicator 1. identifies and compares the physical characteristics of Kansas and the regions of the United States.

Indicator 3. identifies and compares the human characteristics of Kansas and regions of the United States.

Indicator 4. describes the human activities that shape the characteristics of regions (i.e. mining, farming, manufacturing, migration, settlement).

Benchmark 4: Human systems: The student understands how economic, political, cultural, and social processes interact to shape patterns of human populations, interdependence, cooperation, and conflict.

Indicator 2. describes and compares cultural characteristics and patterns within the U.S. (beliefs, customs, food preferences, technology, ways of earning a living).

Indicator 3. identifies factors important in the location of economic activities (population concentration, environmental resources).

Benchmark 5: Human-Environment Interactions: The student understands the effects of interactions between human and physical systems.

Indicator 1. identifies the positive and negative impacts of past, present, and future human activities on the physical environment (loss of habitat, mining, farming, community development).

Indicator 2. identifies ways in which human activities are enhanced or constrained by the physical environment (housing, clothing, recreation, jobs).

Information Power Information Literacy Standards and Indicators: 1.1, 1.2, 1.3, 1.4, 2.1, 2.3, 2.4, 3.2, 3.3, 3.4, 5.1, 5.2, 5.3, 9.1, 9.2, 9.3, 9.4

Cooperative Teaching Plan:

Library Media Specialist Will:

■ Introduce the research project, including notes, bibliographies, and final products.
■ Teach note taking and bibliography skills.
■ Teach the evaluation of sources of information.
■ Guide students in taking notes using phrases rather than sentences.
■ Demonstrate and assist students with note card and bibliography card labeling.
■ Introduce the variety of resources used.
■ Monitor student progress with note taking and bibliography cards.
■ Assess students' notes and bibliography cards.
■ Read rough drafts (with teacher).

Teachers Will:

■ Work with students on creating narratives from the information on their note cards.
■ Assist students in compiling a bibliography page.
■ Monitor class at all times.
■ Introduce float, backpack, and brochure.
■ Introduce outlining in the classroom.
■ Assist students in creating their own outlines with help from the "Fact Finder."

- Read *Scrambled States of America, Wish You Were Here: Emily's Guide to the 50 States,* or *Celebrate the 50 States!* and poems from *My America: A Poetry Atlas of the United States* along with other literature (varies with each teacher) from various regions to introduce unit.
- Monitor student note taking.
- Assess final product using rubric.
- Assign student partners to compare and evaluate resources.
- Read rough drafts (with library media specialist).
- Prepare students for presentations.

Resources:

Print

Fradin, Dennis. *From Sea to Shining Sea* series. Danbury, Connecticut: Children's Press, 1993–1997.

Hopkins, Lee Bennett, ed. *My America: A Poetry Atlas of the United States.* New York: Simon & Schuster, 2000.

Keller, Laurie. *Scrambled States of America.* New York: Henry Holt, 1998.

Krull, Kathleen. *Wish You Were Here: Emily's Guide to the 50 States.* New York: Bantam, 1997.

Leedy, Loreen. *Celebrate the 50 States!* New York: Holiday House, 2000.

Nystrom World Atlas. Chicago: Nystrom, 1999.

World Almanac and Book of Facts 2001. Cleveland: World Almanac Education, 2000.

World Book Encyclopedia. Chicago: World Book, Inc., 2001.

Electronic

Stith, Rebecca. "State Research: Finding Information, READing It, and Using the Information." *Mission Trail Elementary School Library Media Center.* 12 July 2001 <http://www.bv229.k12.ks.us/mtelmc/research.htm>.

Weber, Ray. *50 States.com.* 11 July 2001. 12 July 2001 <www.50states.com>.

Product or Culminating Activity: Students will create a presentation display board, a backpack, a float, and a brochure for their states. Each product affords students the opportunity to synthesize and then creatively utilize the information they have gathered.

Assessment Overview: Teachers assess the presentation display board using the Checklist Assessment. No assessment tool is used to assess the float, brochure, or backpack.

Figure 4.109 State It!

Overview

NAME _____

MY STATE _____

You have been chosen to become an expert for the State of _____. Using the Fact Finder Outline, you will begin your research about your state using various resources. Determine the important aspects about your state that you would like us to know. Look for certain characteristics about your state. Keep all note cards and bibliography cards in designated folders.

OUTLINE:
Using your Fact Finder as a guide, create an outline using the note cards. Please do not use complete sentences.

Now it's time to put all of those facts from your Fact Finder Outline to creative uses! You will create each of the following, using creative thinking skills:

DISPLAY BOARD:
With assistance from the checklist, create a presentation board using information from your outline. It should contain all the information from the checklist including graphs and symbols created in the computer lab. The board should also include the important characteristics you discovered about your state. Be creative! It is your chance to display the important facts about your state.

BACKPACK:
Similar to a backpack you take to school or on a trip, design a backpack for your state. Use a lunch bag-size paper sack given by the teacher. Include at least three symbols from your state.

BROCHURE:
As an expert in your state, you want to entice people to visit your state. Create a brochure with travel information and important visitor sites.

FLOAT:
Get ready for the "Tournament of States Parade" by creating your state's float for this year. Use a shoebox or a box similar in size to create a float displaying an idea or theme from your state.

Figure 4.110   **State It!**

Fact Finder

NAME _____

MY STATE_____

I. Facts in Brief
A. History
Indians
Explorers
Settlers
Year it was settled
Order it entered the Union (USA)
B. Symbols
Nicknames
Flag (describe)
Motto (write English meaning)
Song
Other Symbols
C. Cities
Capital (population and 1 or 2 important
facts)
Five largest (population) cities

II Geography
A. Location
Region
Borders
Absolute points (latitude and longitude)
B. Size
Present population
Rank in population
Racial/Ethnic distribution
Area in square miles
Rank in size
C. Climate
Elevation
Precipitation
Temperature (high, low)
D. Land Regions
Caves
Deserts
Islands
Mountains

Plains
Plateaus
Volcanoes
E. Natural Resources
Animals
Minerals, fuels, stones
Plants (include trees)
Water

III. Economy
A. Agriculture
Crops
Livestock
B. Manufacturing
Machines
Clothing
Technology
C. Mining
Coal
Gold, silver, copper
D. Service (people who help us)
Percentage of people doing this
Examples: Teachers, lawyers, doctors,
dentists, insurance, consultants
Restaurants and retail jobs
E. Tourist Attractions
Sports
Entertainment (theme parks, museums,
theaters, zoos)
Landmarks and monuments
Parks

IV. Famous People

Figure 4.111   State It!

Assessment Checklist: Presentation Display Board Requirements

History (Heading typed and printed): Handwritten and edited paragraph about state history including Indians, Explorers, Settlers, Year Settled, and Order of Entry into the Union. Type and print in the computer lab. Include illustrations to accompany your typed paragraph.

Symbols (Heading typed and printed): Use clipart or drawing and a label for each symbol.

- ❏ Flag (labeled)
- ❏ Seal (labeled)
- ❏ Tree (labeled)
- ❏ Bird (labeled)
- ❏ Flower (labeled)
- ❏ Animal (labeled)
- ❏ Additional one of your choice with typed label

Cities

- ❏ Bar Graph of five largest cities
- ❏ Narrative explaining the graph

Geography

- ❏ Map of the State
- ❏ Include states bordering
- ❏ Labeled bordering state
- ❏ Narrative with location, region, bordering states, and absolute points

Landforms

- ❏ Landform map
- ❏ Label major landforms
- ❏ Brief narrative includes elevation

Climate

- ❏ Table showing high and low temperatures and the amount of precipitation

Natural Resources

- ❏ Clip art or other visual aid of one natural resource
- ❏ Label

Economy

- ❏ Narrative
- ❏ Visual aid describing the state's economy

Famous People

- ❏ Narrative with details about one person from state
- ❏ Illustration

Topics from the North: A Canadian Study

Kristin McIntire, Library Media Specialist
Bob Chaplin, Marlene Hurd, and Jill Farley, Grade 6 Teachers;
Betsy Arntzen, Educational Coordinator, Canadian-American Center,
University of Maine, Orono
Conners-Emerson School
11 Eagle Lake Road, Bar Harbor, ME 04609
207-288-5708
kmcintire@u98.k12.me.us

Grade Level: 6

Unit Overview: The primary goal of Topics from the North: A Canadian Study is students' improved understanding of our northern neighbor through exploration of contemporary and historical Canadian topics. We encourage students to gain knowledge from their own research and that of their peers on people, places, or events in historical or present day Canada; work through the information skills process in order to experience true research and create a research-based end product; and present their research findings through a poster and a presentation. A strength of the unit is the variety of topics students can research, representing a number of interests and levels of difficulty, thus making the unit easily modified and extended for students.

Time Frame: 4 weeks (This unit follows a social studies teaching unit on Canada. After students have knowledge concerning the geography, history, culture, and economics of Canada and her provinces, they begin work on the research component of their study.)

Content Area Standards: State of Maine Learning Results
<http://www.state.me.us/education/lres/lres.htm>

English Language Arts, Middle Grades 5–8
Standard D. Informational Texts: Students will apply reading, listening, and viewing strategies in informational texts across all areas of curriculum.
D.1 Seek appropriate assistance when attempting to comprehend challenging text.
D.2 Identify useful information organizing strategies.
D.4 Identify different ways in which informational texts are organized.
D.6 Describe new knowledge presented in informational texts and how it can be used.
D.8 Use the various parts of a text (index, table of contents, glossary) to locate specific information.

Standard H. Research Related Writing and Speaking: Students will work, write, and speak effectively when researching all content areas.
H.1 Collect and synthesize data for research topics from interviews and field work, using note taking and other appropriate strategies.

H.2 Separate information collected for research topics into major components based on relevant criteria.

H.3 Create bibliographies.

H.4 Use available catalogs to locate materials for research reports.

H.5 Use indexes to periodical literature to locate information for research.

H.6 Use magazines, newspapers, dictionaries, journal, and other print sources to gather information for research topics.

H.7 Use search engines and other Internet resources to collect information for research topics.

Social Studies, Middle Grades 5–8

History: Students will learn to analyze the human experience through time, to recognize the relationships of events and people, and to identify patterns, themes, and turning points of change using the chronology of history and major eras. In interpreting current and historical events, students will evaluate the credibility and perspectives of multiple sources of information gathered from technology, documents, artifacts, maps, the arts, and literature.

Standard C. Historical Inquiry, Analysis, and Interpretation: Students will learn to evaluate resource material such as documents, artifacts, maps, artworks, and literature, and to make judgments about the perspectives of the authors and their credibility when interpreting current historical events.

H.1 Judge the accuracy of historical fiction by comparing the characters and events described with descriptions in multiple primary sources.

H.3 Use information from a variety of primary and secondary sources to identify and support a point of view on a controversial historical topic.

H.5 Formulate historical questions based on examination of primary and secondary sources including documents, eyewitness accounts, letters and diaries, artifacts, real or simulated historical sites, charts, graphs, diagrams, and written texts.

Information Power Information Literacy Standards and Indicators: 1.1, 1.2, 1.3, 1.4, 1.5, 2.1, 2.2, 2.3, 2.4, 3.2, 3.2, 3.3, 3.4

Cooperative Teaching Plan:

Library Media Specialist Will:

- Secure resources from Canadian-American Center at the University of Maine <http://www.umaine.edu/canam/> including vertical files of travel brochures, clippings from Canadian newspapers, URLs, and videos.
- Schedule no less than three periods during week one for students to begin project.
- Review Research Guidelines and Bibliography format with students.
- Play Research Process Game to introduce Research Guidelines.
- Provide a brief overview of the unit (with teachers).
- Discuss potential questions, explaining that the place, people, or event tag is simply a recommendation.
- Share reference resources and books in the circulating collection.
- Supervise and assist in student research (with teachers).

Teachers Will:

- Prepare students for Canada research by teaching a unit on Canada.
- Prepare handouts for students.
- Supervise student assignment of partners and topics.
- Give a brief overview of the unit (with library media specialist).
- Review the Poster Rubric with students for clarification.
- Supervise and assist in student research (with library media specialist).
- Assess student work with the Poster Rubric and the Research Rubric (whenever possible with library media specialist).

Resources:

Print

Department of Canadian Heritage. *Symbols of Canada.* Ottawa: Canadian Government Publishing, 1999. (Available for $9.95 from Canadian Government Publishing, Public Works and Government, Services Canada, Ottawa, ON Canada K1A 0S9; 1-800-635-7943.)

Gall, Timothy L. and Susan Bevan Gall, eds. *Junior Worldmark Encyclopedia of the Canadian Provinces.* Detroit: UXL, 1997.

Greenwood, Barbara. *The Kids Book of Canada: Exploring the Land and the People.* Buffalo, New York: Kids Can Press, 1997.

Hello Canada series. Minneapolis: Lerner Publications, 1995.

*Jones, Charlotte Foltz. *Yukon Gold: The Story of the Klondike Gold Rush.* New York: Holiday House, 1999. (Klondike Gold Rush, Yukon)

*Kizilos, Peter. *Quebec: A Province Divided.* Minneapolis: Lerner Publications, 2000. (Separatism, Quebec)

Let's Discover Canada series. New York: Chelsea House, 1991.

*Livesey, Robert and A.G. Smith. *The Fur Traders.* New York: Stoddard Kids, 1998. (Hudson Bay Company, past and present, Northwest Territories)

*McFarlane, Brian. *Hockey for Kids: Heroes, Tips, and Facts.* New York: Beech Tree, 1996. (Hockey, Ontario)

Pang, Guek-Chang. *Canada.* New York: Marshall Cavendish, 1996.

Peoples of the Americas: Volume 3, Canada-Cayman Islands. New York: Marshall Cavendish, 1999.

*Siska, Heather Smith. *People of the Ice: How the Inuit Lived.* Buffalo, NY: Firefly Books, 1995.
(Inuit Culture, Nunavut)

*Wallace, Mary. *The Inuksuk Book.* Toronto: Owl Books, 1999. (Tundra/Standing Stones, Nunavut)

*Selected Topical Resources (especially good/useful for selected topics)

Electronic

Bennett, M. D. "Teaching and Learning About Canada: Resources for Teachers and Students." *Teaching and Learning about Canada.* 24 July 2001 <http://www.canadainfolink.ca/teach.htm>.

Calgary Stampede. 24 July 2001 <http://www.calgarystampede.com/stampede>. (Calgary Stampede, Alberta)

Carnaval de Quebec. 24 July 2001 <http://www.carnaval.qc.ca/menueng.htm>. (Winter Carnival, Quebec)

Confederation Bridge. 24 July 2001 <http://www.confederationbridge.com/>. (Confederation Bridge, Prince Edward Island)

Fortress of Louisburg. 24 July 2001 <http://fortress.uccb.ns.ca/>. (Fort Louisburg, Nova Scotia)

"Grey Owl Biography." Virtual Saskatchewan: On-line Magazine. 24 July 2001 <http://www.virtualsk.com/current_issue/grey_owl_bio.html>. (Grey Owl, Saskatchewan)

Ramirez, Alice. "Churchill, Canada." Explorations: Homepage of Alice Ramierez. 24 July 2001 <http://www.chem.ucla.edu/~alice/explorations/churchill/cindex.htm>. (Churchill and the Polar Bears, Manitoba)

"Teaching Canada." *University of Maine.* 24 July 2001 <http://www.umaine.edu/canam/teachingcanada.htm>.

*Selected Topical Web sites (especially useful for topics lacking adequate print sources)

Product or Culminating Activity: Students make class presentations using posters as visual aides, as well as any other supporting materials

Assessment Overview: Rubrics include Poster Rubric, Research Rubric, and Research Process Score Sheet (a score sheet that teacher or library media specialist may use to score research process in the library and the classroom). The assessments are ideally a joint effort between the student, teacher, and LMS. Practically, we have found that it is the teacher who does the bulk of the scoring. This is partly because our library is not on a fully flexible schedule and it has been impossible to coordinate presentation times with the library media specialist's free periods.

Adaptations and Extensions: The topics are not assigned randomly. As students show an interest in a particular province or subject during the teaching unit, matches can be made or new topics created. For instance, a gifted student was especially interested in the James Bay Hydro Project. The engineering aspect drew him to that topic, and so we added it. Some topics are easier to handle than others because of the straightforwardness or abundance of resources. These topics are usually assigned to students who are weaker academically.

| Figure 4.112 | Topics from the North: A Canadian Study |

Research Process Game: Instructions for Library Media Specialists and Teachers

This simple game encourages student involvement and understanding when introducing the research process.

Supplies:

Prepare an envelope for each student containing index cards with the six steps of the research process printed on them:

Presearch	Search	Interpret and Evaluate Information
Plan Presentation	Make Presentation	Evaluate Project

To Play:

Ask students to put the cards in order based on what they understand about researching. Some of the words (such as *Interpret* and *Evaluate*) may be unfamiliar, so some explanation of what they mean may be necessary.

Once everyone has had time to put his/her cards in order, ask for suggestions of the proper order.

Now, write the correct answers on a board or overhead. Explain each step along the way, and give examples of the kinds of activities that are involved. Encourage students to reorder their strips as needed.

[Note: The first three steps (Presearch, Search, Interpret and Evaluate Information) are what I have dubbed the "rabbit steps." After drawing a picture of a bunny, tell the class that they will hop back and forth between these steps.]

After all of the steps are explained and listed correctly, erase the board. Students should now mix up their steps and reorder them correctly. You can make it into a contest between tables, groups, or individual students.

Figure 4.113 | **Topics from the North: A Canadian Study**

Research Guidelines

Step One: Presearch
- Make a list of what you already know about your topic and check to see if you are right.
- If you don't know anything about your topic, look it up in a general resource, like an encyclopedia or a book.
- Ask yourself questions about the topic you are studying and write them down.
- Create a plan for the search. Where will you look for information? What key words or search phrases will you use? Write down your ideas.

Remember, you can always come back to this step (and you will probably have to as you get into the actual search for information)!

Ideas for places to look:

library catalog   computer databases   periodicals   newspapers

letters   specialized encyclopedias   surveys   interviews

nonprint materials   atlases and globes   generalencyclopedias   almanacs

Step Two: Search
- Find the information that you planned to look for in your presearch.
- If you get stuck, ask the library media specialist or your teacher for help.
- Keep track of the resources you use for a bibliography.
- Check your progress and decide if you need to go back to the presearch step to ask more questions or brainstorm more search ideas.

You will probably do the next step, Interpret and Evaluate, at the same time as the Search step, and that is fine!

Step Three: Interpret and Evaluate Information
- Read the questions you brainstormed and ask yourself, "Which question does this information answer?"
- Skim the information to find the parts that answer your questions.
- Read your information and ask yourself, "What is this about?" Write about it in your own words (paraphrase), and then reread to make sure you got it right.
- Read your information a third time to look for new key words that you could use in a search related to your topic. List your new key words on your brainstorming sheet.
- Check your progress and decide if you need to go back to the presearch step to ask more questions, or to the search step to find more information.

Figure 4.113   (continued from page 200)

Step Four: Prepare your presentation

■ Decide on the best way to present your knowledge (a paper, poster, multimedia, movie, oral talk, or other ideas).

■ Decide how you will start. Write a short paragraph telling what your project or paper will show.

■ Gather all of your information and organize it to fit the format you chose to use. (If you are writing a paper, you should follow the steps of the writing process.)

■ Create and use appropriate visuals to make your paper or project stronger.

■ Talk to your classroom teacher or library media specialist if you need help or more ideas.

Step Five: Make your presentation

■ Make a clear and accurate presentation in the format you selected.

Step Six: Evaluate your project

■ Think about your resources. Which ones were most useful?

■ Think about how well you did going through the research process according to this guide.

■ Think about how much and what you learned.

■ Ask your classmates and teachers to evaluate your project.

Figure 4.114 Topics from the North: A Canadian Study

Research Topics

TOPIC	PROVINCE	TYPE
Temperate Rainforest	British Columbia	place
Totem Poles	British Columbia	people
Dinosaurs-Tyrrell Museum of Paleontology	Alberta	place
Calgary Stampede	Alberta	event
Grey Owl	Saskatchewan	people
Ethnic Groups and Wheat Growers	Saskatchewan	people
Churchill and Polar Bears	Manitoba	place
Banff National Park	Manitoba	place
Royal Canadian Mounted Police (headquarters)	Ontario	people
Great Lakes and Population of Canada	Ontario	place
Hockey	Ontario	event
St. Lawrence Seaway	Quebec	place
Winter Carnival	Quebec	event
Separatism	Quebec	people
Acadians-Evangeline	Nova Scotia	people
Loyalists	Nova Scotia	people
Fort Louisburg	Nova Scotia	place
Cape Breton Island and Celtic Culture	Nova Scotia	place
Mi'kmaqs	New Brunswick	people
City of Saint John	New Brunswick	place
Vikings	Newfoundland	people
Codfisheries	Newfoundland	people
Hudson Bay Company, past and present	Northwest Territories	people
Canadian Culture in Yellowknife	Northwest Territories	place
Klondike (Gold Rush)	Yukon	event
Kluane National Park	Yukon	place
Confederation Bridge	PEI	event
Anne of Green Gables, Lucy Maud Montgomery	PEI	event
Inuit's Culture	Nunevut	people
Tundra and Standing Stones	Nunevut	place

| Figure 4.115 | Topics from the North: A Canadian Study |

Five Possible Questions

You may wish to choose five questions to focus your research on from the list of questions below. If so, circle your choices. Or, you may use these questions as a starting place, borrowing only one or two and writing the rest of the questions on your own. Remember, to earn the highest score for the project you must ask and answer eight questions in total!

Place

1. Who explored this area? Who were the immigrants (the people who originally settled this area)?
2. What are the physical features of this place? Do the physical features influence how and why people live here? Explain.
3. What is the system of government? Why did they choose this system of government?
4. What customs and traditions exist today that may have been brought by settlers? (e.g. farming techniques, fishing methods, holiday family celebrations)
5. What are the natural resources here and how are they being used?

People

1. How did the physical features help or prevent the exploration of this area by your people?
2. How were the native people treated by the immigrants?
3. What customs and traditions exist today that may have been brought by settlers? (e.g. farming techniques, fishing methods, holiday family celebrations)
4. In what ways have the life styles changed for native peoples in the Arctic— the Inuit— and for native peoples in the west, such as the Metis, in the last 150 years?
5. What were the issues and goals of the explorers? What did they want at this time in history?

Events

1. Why and when did your event take place? Why did it happen?
2. Who were the leaders of Canada during this historical event? What part did the leaders play in this event?
3. What consequences are evident today as a result of this event? How is life different? How was the "common man" affected by this great event?
4. What other events were happening in the world at this time?
5. Did the fact that Canada and the United States were neighbors play a part in this event?

Figure 4.116 Topics from the North: A Canadian Study

Reference Response Sheet

Bibliographic Information	What Question?	Comments

Figure 4.117 **Topics from the North: A Canadian Study**

Poster Rubric

	Graphics	Shared Required Information	Presentation
4	-easy to understand visuals: props, pictures, drawings, or maps -shows clear and important relationship to topic information	-demonstrates complete knowledge of five required questions and asks and answers at least three more	-continuous eye contact and clear voice throughout -shared knowledge beyond required information -well organized and understandable presentation
3	-understandable visuals: props, pictures, drawings, or maps -graphics relate to information on topic	-demonstrates good knowledge of five required questions and asks and answers at least one more	-good eye contact and clear voice throughout most of presentation -shared knowledge of all required information -organized and understandable throughout most of presentation.
2	-difficult to understand visuals that may not relate to information about topic	-demonstrates some knowledge of five required questions	-eye contact and clear voice throughout most of presentation. -shared knowledge of more than half of required information. -organized and understandable during some of presentation.
1	unclear visuals that have no apparent relationship to information on topic	-demonstrates poor knowledge of three or four out of five required questions	-little eye contact and unclear voice throughout presentation. -shared knowledge of less than half of required information. -organized and understandable during some of presentation.
0	-no visuals -visuals are completely unrelated to topic	-demonstrates poor knowledge of fewer than three required questions	-no eye contact and unclear voice through-out presentation. -shared no information -not organized or understandable

Figure 4.118 Topics from the North: A Canadian Study

Research Rubric

	Followed Research Process (ongoing)	Evidence of Paraphrased Material	Reference Response Sheet
4	-completely follows research guidelines -shows clear evidence of a plan and order in research	-has well organized notes with well written, detailed paraphrased material	-records every source in detail using all three columns.
3	-closely follows research guidelines - shows evidence of a plan and order in research	-has well organized notes with well written paraphrased material	-records most sources in detail using all three columns.
2	-follows research guidelines - shows some evidence of a plan and order in research	-has organized notes with some paraphrased material	-records the majority of sources in detail using all three columns.
1	-barely follows research guidelines - shows little evidence of a plan and order in research	-has confusing notes with no paraphrased material.	-records few sources in some detail using all three columns
0	-did not follow research guidelines - shows no evidence of a plan and order in research	-demonstrates poor knowledge of fewer than three required questions	-records fewer than two sources in some detail without using all columns.

Figure 4.119 Topics from the North: A Canadian Study

Research Process Score Sheet

The process you follow throughout the project
will be scored with the following criteria

_____ Follow the research process
■ see research guidelines
■ check off each step as you complete it

_____ Show evidence of paraphrased information through notes
■ keep notes together throughout research

_____ Complete final draft of note cards
■ remember grammar, punctuation, spelling
■ show good organization

_____ Complete Reference Response Sheet
■ use all three columns
■ record every resource

_____ Complete Work Timeline each day with a logical plan

You will turn in the following items from your research at the end of the unit:
■ research guidelines with checkmarks
■ original notes
■ reference response sheet
■ work timeline
■ poster and presentation

Note: Your teacher will fill this score sheet out during the research process. The points assigned will be based on the Research Rubric.

Unsolved Mysteries

Dana Davis-Avants, Librarian
Vicki Hanson, Sixth Grade Reading and Social Studies
Win Hageman, Grade 6 Computer Teacher
Tannahill Intermediate School
701 American Flyer Blvd., Fort Worth, TX 76108
817-367-1370
ddavisavants@esc11.net

Grade Level: 6

Unit Overview: Unsolved Mysteries is a mind-boggling unit that leads students away from traditional topics used for teaching vocabulary, comprehension, research, and writing, and into the unknown. Students research a mysterious topic in order to gain information to form a fact-based opinion, then complete a written report and drawing. The library media specialist, reading teacher, and computer teacher collaborate to ensure student success. Students learn note taking, Web searching, and organization of information to create a written report supporting the facts and their own opinions. Drawings are presented and displayed on hall bulletin boards. Extension lessons continue the mysterious topics to make reading an enjoyable and engrossing subject.

Time Frame: 4 weeks (including Extension Activities)

Content Area Standards: Texas Essential Knowledge Skills (TEKS)
<http://www.tea.state.tx.us/teks/>

English Language Arts and Reading, Grade 6

6.9 Reading Vocabulary Development: The student acquires an extensive vocabulary through reading and systematic word study.
C. use multiple reference aids, including a thesaurus, a synonym finder, a dictionary, and software, to clarify meanings and usage.

6.10 Reading Comprehension: The student comprehends selections using a variety of strategies.
B. establish and adjust purposes for reading such as reading to find out, to understand, to interpret, to enjoy, and to solve problems (4-8);
E. use the text's structure or progression of ideas such as cause and effect or chronology to locate and recall information;
F. determine a text's main (or major ideas) and how those ideas are supported with details;
G. paraphrase and summarize text to recall, inform, or organize ideas;
H. draw inferences such as conclusions or generalizations and support them with text evidence and experience;
J. distinguish fact and opinion in various texts (4-8);
L. represent text information in different ways such as in outline, timeline, or graphic organizer.

6.11 Reading Literary Response: The student expresses and supports responses to various types of texts.

A. offer observations, make connections, react, speculate, interpret, and raise questions in response to texts;

C. support responses by referring to relevant aspects of text and his/her own experiences;

D. connect, compare, and contrast ideas, themes, and issues across text.

6.12 Reading/Text Structures: The student analyzes the characteristics of various types of texts (genres).

A. identify the purposes of different types of texts such as to inform, influence, express, or entertain;

H. describe how the author's perspective or point of view affects the text;

K. recognize how style, tone, and mood contribute to the effect of the text.

Information Power Information Literacy Standards and Indicators: 1.1, 1.2, 1.3, 1.4, 1.5, 2.1, 2.2, 2.3, 2.4, 3.1, 3.2, 3.3

Cooperative Teaching Plan:

Librarian Will:

■ Review the research process from topic selection to information access and presentation.

■ Review speech skills, those things to remember when doing an oral presentation.

■ Present an overview of resources available in the library.

■ Assist students with individual research.

■ Provide a cart of books and resources located by students for continued classroom use.

Classroom Teacher Will:

■ Introduce unit in the classroom

■ Read *The Lake Worth Monster* by Sallie Ann Clarke plus newspaper articles to discuss local unsolved mysteries. (Any unsolved mystery books or articles could be used.)

■ Discuss what an unsolved mystery is and what topics are available for research.

■ Evaluate information and presentation.

■ Supervise cooperative learning groups in extension activity.

Computer Teacher Will:

■ Find and bookmark sites that are appropriate for student research.

■ Assist students in researching Web sites, taking notes, and printing needed information.

Resources:

Print

*Billings, Henry and Melissa. *Phenomena: 21 Extraordinary Stories—with Exercises for Developing Critical Reading Skills*. Lincolnwood, Illinois: Jamestown Publishers, 1984.

Cavendish, Richard. *Men, Myth and Magic: The Illustrated Encyclopedia of Mythology, Religion and the Unknown*. Tarrytown, New York: Marshall Cavendish, 1995.

Clarke, Sallie Ann. *The Lake Worth Monster*. Fort Worth, Texas: n.p.,1969

*Dramer, Dan. Monsters: *21 Stories of the Most Fantastic and Gruesome Creatures of All*

Times—With Exercises for Developing Critical Thinking. Lincolnwood, Illinois: Jamestown Publishers, 1985.

Great Mysteries Opposing Viewpoints Series (Titles include: *ESP, Bigfoot,* and *Pyramids*). San Diego: Greenhaven Press, Inc.

Mysteries of Mind, Space & Time: The Unexplained. New York: H.S. Stuttman Inc., 1992.

Mysteries of Science Series (Titles include *UFOs, Yeti: Abominable Snowman of the Himalayas,* and *Near-Death Experiences*). Brookfield, Connecticut: Millbrook Press.

*Warner, John F. and Warner, Margaret B. *Aliens & UFO's: 21 Famous UFO Sightings—With Exercises for Developing Critical Reading Skills.* Lincolnwood, Illinois: Jamestown Publishers, 1994.

*Warner, John F. and Margaret B. Warner. *Apparitions: 21 Stories of Ghost, Spirits, and Mysterious Manifestations—With Exercises for Developing Critical Thinking Skills.* Lincolnwood, Illinois: Jamestown Publishers, 1987.

Electronic

Searches are conducted for two days in the computer lab. It should be noted that the classroom teacher and computer teacher suggest searching only bookmarked sites due to oddities and somewhat inappropriate sites encountered when searching these topics. Bookmarked sites include:

"Encyclopedia Smithsonian: The Loch Ness Monster." *Smithsonian Institution.* 22 July 2001 <http://www.si.edu/resource/faq/nmnh/lochness.htm >.

Gibson, Tobias. "The Bermuda Triangle." *Blind Kat Publishers.* 22 July 2001 <http://blindkat.tripod.com/triangle/tri.html>

The Museum of Unnatural Mystery. 22 July 2001 <www.unmuseum.org>.

"Stephen Hawking's Universe Unsolved Mysteries." *PBS.* 22 July 2001. 22 July 2001 <http://www.pbs.org/wnet/hawking/mysteries/html/myst.html >.

Product or Culminating Activity:

Each student will write a five paragraph paper following a supplied outline. He/She will create a drawing on his/her topic which includes the words "Unsolved Mysteries" and a colorful picture to describe the topic. Volunteers may orally present to the class on their topic.

Assessment Overview:

Written report and drawing are assessed by the classroom teacher using rubrics for each.

Adaptations and Extensions:

Cooperative groups of three to four students do an assigned daily reading from the starred books in the resources section above. They discuss the story in their cooperative groups and make an oral presentation to the class summarizing the story. Each group is evaluated using the grade strips. The teacher uses the grade strip to write comments while groups are working and interacting. Each group may build to 100 points.

Students independently complete the "How Well Did You Read?" worksheet (found at the end of each story in the books) for their story. Each has four sections: 1) Finding the Main Idea; 2) Recalling Facts; 3) Making Inferences; 4) Using Words Precisely. Each section is scored and totaled for a critical reading total score.

Figure 4.120   **Unsolved Mysteries**

Essay Outline

I.   Introduction
■ Explain your unsolved mystery in five sentences.

II. Controversy
■ Offer different possibilities/reasons why people *think* it happened.

III. Facts
■ Tell what we know for certain.

IV. Your Opinion
■ Offer three reasons why you made up your mind.
■ Explain each of the three reasons the mystery could or could not have happened/existed.

V.   Conclusion
■ Restate your introduction in other words.
■ Think of a *"clincher"* ending.

Unsolved Mystery Topics

Elvis's Death	Mind Power	Amelia Earhart
Hollow Earth	Roanoke Island	Healers
Atlantis	Siberian Fireball	Sphinx
Stonehenge	Acupuncture	Dinosaurs
Vampires	UFO's/Aliens	Crop Circles
Afterlife	Nostradamos	Bermuda Triangle
Precognition	Reincarnation	Great Pyramids
Ghosts	Abominable Snowman	Time Travel
People Without Pain	Meaning of Dreams	Sasquatch/Big Foot
Loch Ness Monster	Evolution	Angels
Zombies	Déjà vu	Death of JFK
Lines of Nazca	Easter Island	The Mary Celeste
	Spontaneous Human Combustion	

Figure 4.121   **Unsolved Mysteries**

Essay Rubric

Name_____

Topic_____

I.   **Introduction (Paragraph #1):** Contains at least five sentences and gives the reader a good overview of the unsolved mystery.
Comments:

_____ points (out of 20)

II.   **Controversy (Paragraph #2):** Offers at least three different possibilities/reasons why people *think* it happened.
Comments:

_____ points (out of 20)

III.   **Facts (Paragraph #3):** States and explains at least five facts researched and known for certain.
Comments:

_____ points (out of 20)

IV.   **Your Opinion (Paragraph #4):** Offers three reasons why you made up your mind as you did and explains each of the three reasons the mystery could or could not have happened.
Comments:

_____ points (out of 20)

V.   **Conclusion:** Restates your introduction in other words and draws the essay to a conclusion. Includes a *"clincher"* ending or statement to entice the reader to do further research.
Comments:

_____ points (out of 20)

        TOTAL SCORE _____ (out of 100)

Figure 4.122   **Unsolved Mysteries**

Drawing Rubric

Name_____

Topic_____

I.   Includes the words "Unsolved Mysteries" incorporated into the drawing.
Comments:

_____ points (out of 30)

II.   Drawing represents and/or describes the topic.
Comments:

_____ points (out of 30)

III.   Good use of color in the drawing.
Comments:

_____ points (out of 30)

IV.   Overall presentation and appropriate size (8½"× 11")
Comments:

_____ points (out of 10)

TOTAL SCORE _____ (out of 100)

Figure 4.123   **Unsolved Mysteries**

Grade Strip

Note: Grade Strips are used to grade cooperative learning groups in an extension activity. There are four students in each group. On the back of the Grade Strip, each student in your group should write his/her name and job (see the list; jobs will change each day as you change groups). Be sure to include the title of your reading at the top. The teacher will write comments on Grade Strips while your groups are working and interacting. Each group may build to 100 points.

Jobs
Leader: Reads the three page passage about the unsolved mystery topic.
Recorder: Writes down the facts gained from the reading and the opinions, comments, and conclusions of the group.
Speaker: Presents an overview of the reading, the facts, and the opinions formed by the group.
Sargent at Arms/Peacemaker: Directs the discussion of the group and mediates.

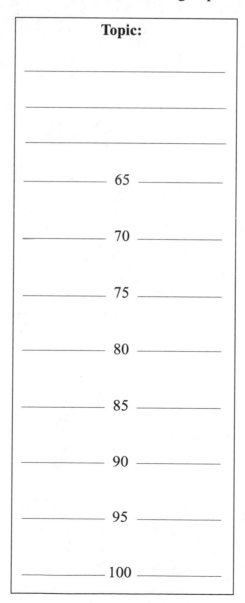

Index